OSMAR WHITE

CONQUERORS' *Road*

OSMAR WHITE

CONQUERORS' *Road*

CAMBRIDGE
UNIVERSITY PRESS

PUBLISHED BY THE PRESS SYNDICATE OF THE UNIVERSITY OF CAMBRIDGE
The Pitt Building, Trumpington Street, Cambridge, United Kingdom

CAMBRIDGE UNIVERSITY PRESS
The Edinburgh Building, Cambridge CB2 2RU, UK
40 West 20th Street, New York, NY 10011–4211, USA
477 Williamstown Road, Port Melbourne, VIC 3207, Australia
Ruiz de Alarcón 13, 28014 Madrid, Spain
Dock House, The Waterfront, Cape Town 8001, South Africa

http://www.cambridge.org

© Sally White 1996

This book is in copyright. Subject to statutory exception
and to the provisions of relevant collective licensing agreements,
no reproduction of any part may take place without
the written permission of Cambridge University Press.

First published by HarperCollinsPublishers 1996
This edition published by Cambridge University Press 2003

Printed in the United States of America

Typeface Palatino (*Adobe*) 9.5/12 pt.   *System* QuarkXPress®

A catalogue record for this book is available from the British Library

National Library of Australia Cataloguing in Publication data
White, Osmar, 1909–1991.
Conquerors' road.
Bibliography.
Includes index.
ISBN 0521 53751 7 (pbk).
ISBN 0 521 83051 6
1. United States. Army. Army, 3rd. 2. World War, 1939–1945
– Campaigns – Germany. 3. Germany – History – 1945–1955.
I. Title.
940.54213

ISBN 0 521 53751 7 paperback
ISBN 0 521 83051 6 hardback

For Jeremy, Pierz and Randal

'Arrows show where Allied armies are thrusting deeply beyond
the Rhine. Shaded area indicates the depth of the latest advances.'
Map accompanying one of White's dispatches, 1945

Contents

When the armor turned west along the Autoba[n]
from Hersfeld someone said; "Well, this is the concentrat[ion]
camp country." True.

Wolmar fell. A woman who claimed to have an Ameri[can]
mother interpreted for the burgomaster when he was being
interrogated after surrender. Later she answered quest[ions]
for the Press. In a shrill, superior voice she harped
about the little city's great cultural tradition, and it[s]
claim to special consideration. as the home of Go[ethe]
Schiller and Liszt.

"Of course," she complained, "your bombers always
managed to hit some cultural edifice!"

My billet was in a rich home near the park where Li[szt's]
garden cottage stands. It was full of solid, comfortab[le]
furniture. It had well stocked book shelves, a garden

had been lovingly tended. It seemed to have belonged [to]
an educated and reflective man — a stodgy man perha[ps]
but one who used life's good things with decent moderat[ion].
Over the bed in my room was a colored print of

Page from White's original manuscript

Editors' Note

At the end of *Green Armour*, his classic account of his experiences during the New Guinea Campaign, Osmar White describes how a 500-pound bomb struck the tank-landing ship on which he was leaving Rendova Harbour in the central Solomons. The four men standing beside him in the wheelhouse were killed. 'Why these four men should have died and I live and walk, I do not know,' White wrote. 'But I know this. The living have the cause of the dead in trust. The cause of the dead was the defence of what they believed to be truth, justice and decency.'

White's words were not mere rhetoric. He believed wholeheartedly in the Allied cause in the Second World War. But he did not gloss over the failings of his own side. Despite tight military censorship, his dispatches from New Guinea exposed the Australians' inadequate training in jungle warfare. With ABC broadcaster Chester Wilmot and Department of Information cameraman Damien Parer he campaigned to get the army to adopt green uniforms. It was on his and Parer's advice that the US Army decided to camouflage its uniforms by dyeing them a mottled green. Yet when he ventured a strong opinion, it was based always on what he had observed as a reporter in the field, as both *Green Armour* and *Conquerors' Road* amply demonstrate.

Green Armour was written in Australia in late 1943 while White regained the use of his legs, shattered by the Japanese bomb. Clearly his days of jungle warfare were over but his boss at the *Herald & Weekly Times*, Sir Keith Murdoch, wanted him back in the field. By August 1944, White was in New York; in September he was in England, investigating British industry and the morale of the British people. By the first week in November, he had reached Paris and was sending dispatches from Supreme Allied Command in the liberated French capital.

Late in February 1945, he joined the United States Twelfth Army Group — which included the Third Army under George Patton — on the Western Front. He remained attached to the Third Army as it swept north and east through Germany.

Conquerors' Road is based on the notes and articles White wrote while covering those final months of war and the first months of the Allied occupation of Germany. Many of his European dispatches were picked up by British and American papers and enhanced his international reputation, a reputation largely based on the success of *Green Armour*, which had been enthusiastically received in both Britain and the United States.

As White explains in his 1983 introduction, *Conquerors' Road* too was at first well received by his British and American publishers. They listed it for publication in the northern spring of 1946 but then mysteriously cancelled publication without explanation. Consequently when he unearthed the manuscript in the early 1980s it was unedited. So, like any good professional, White revised and polished his work.

These revisions, however, posed some problems for his editors. Was he influenced in his assessments by the voluminous literature on the war and its aftermath that had appeared since the Armistice? After a careful examination of the original copy, the answer is 'no'.

White was able to retain the original tenor of *Conquerors' Road* so effortlessly because, unlike those who have continued to research and write about the period, he put the war behind him. Although he made his name as a war correspondent, he never defined himself as such. As a result, he absorbed very little of the post-war histories and memoirs. He read his friend Chester Wilmot's *The Struggle for Europe* but not much else.

With one exception, the revisions are based firmly on the 1945 manuscript. Most are the kind of minor changes that would have occurred had the manuscript gone through a normal pre-publication revision. Sometimes White compressed his text severely. More rarely he added minor background detail to help a generation of readers who had not recently lived through the war. Only the moving conclusion did not appear in the original manuscript; it is, however, completely in the spirit of the original.

White also cut original material where he felt it was holding up the narrative. Some of these passages proved so interesting as historical source material that they appear in the appendices along with the original introduction and conclusion. We have also incorporated, as appendices, examples of White's dispatches as they appeared in Australian newspapers. The story of the return of the Sudeten Germans covers events largely ignored by historians, while his emotional dispatch on Buchenwald makes a fascinating contrast with his description of the same events in the book.

White's other main revision was to restructure the order of the chapters. Since the content remains virtually the same in both texts, there seems little point in spelling out the original structure.

Even though *Conquerors' Road* is surprisingly frank for a book written in 1945, White does exclude some information. He may have known about General Patton's practice of clearing battlefields of the American dead but leaving the rotting German corpses to be seen by the fresh US troops although he does not refer to it, perhaps because at the time he was unable to verify the practice to his professional satisfaction. Some idea of White's reaction to Patton's style, however, is contained in the passages expressing disgust at the general's 'preoccupation with corpses' during press conferences.

Similarly White's account of Colonel Charles Keegan's failure to implement the de-Nazification program in Bavaria does not explain its implications for General Patton. In fact, this was one of a series of incidents that ultimately led to Patton's removal as Military Governor of Bavaria. It is probable that White was unable to pursue the story personally as he had left Germany before Eisenhower decided to fire Patton. These minor limitations notwithstanding, *Conquerors' Road* contains much that will be new to modern readers and historians of post-war Europe.

The book brings to life some of the most significant events of this century in the vivid prose of a master of reportage.

What is not so clear from the text, however, is the profound effect that White's experiences in the shattered Germany had on him. Once, when asked why as a senior writer for the Melbourne *Herald* he had pursued a long and emotionally exhausting campaign to reform child welfare and mental health provisions in Victoria in the early 1950s, White replied:

'I was walking down Collins Street soon after I came back from Europe and I looked at all the ordinary faces. Ordinary people had allowed the obscenity of Nazism to develop and they pleaded ignorance when faced with the results of their actions or lack of action. I realised then we were as capable as they had been of appalling acts if we pleaded ignorance of the seemingly small injustices all around us. Ignorance allows small injustices to grow into inhumanity.'

In New Guinea, White had seen the nobility of ordinary men fighting in almost unbearable and primitive conditions. In Germany, he saw the results of the depravity of ordinary people. For nearly two decades after the war, he spent much of his time in Papua New Guinea as the *Herald*'s special correspondent in the region. He never returned to Germany.

Sally A. White
Neil McDonald
February 1996

Osmar White, December 1944
Photographer: unknown

Author's Note

Although this book deals with the invasion and occupation of Nazi Germany by the armies of the Western Allies in 1945, it does not purport to be war history in the accepted sense of the term. Nor is it a considered critique of performance by military governments set up to control the defeated nation after its unconditional surrender in May that year. It is merely a record of the personal observations and reflections of one man who was privileged as a civilian war correspondent to witness historical events rather than reconstruct them from documentary and other sources at a later date. It does not depend on recollection, but on facts and impressions set down in writing at the time of their happening.

Most of the text was drafted between January and November 1945 while I was working in the field as a reporter for a syndicate of Australian and British newspapers. The material was an expansion and elaboration of diary notes and incorporated press dispatches which had suffered at the hands of military censors.

When mandatory censorship was lifted at the end of the war, I collated and edited what I had written to conform to a theme covered by the title *Conquerors' Road* and sent it to the London and New York publishing houses which had earlier that year published the hardcover editions of *Green Armour*, my book about the early campaigns against the Japanese in New Guinea and the Solomon Islands. Both firms had invited me to submit for consideration any similar work I might produce about my experience in Europe.

Conquerors' Road still lacked its final chapters, but the reaction of the British publishers, Unwin Hyman, was enthusiastic. They advised me that, as the subject matter was so topical, they proposed to expedite publication and asked me to complete the manuscript urgently as the chapters already to hand had been typeset. An advance against royalties had been approved and a contract awaited my signature in London.

At this time, however, my Australian employers had arranged for me to return to Melbourne by air and my stopover in London was too brief for me to do more than check galley proofs of material in type and provide a synopsis of what I had yet to write.

In January I finished the job and mailed the text to London and the American publishers, W. W. Norton. About six weeks later the senior editor at Norton's wrote to inform me that 'after long consideration management has decided with deep regret that *Conquerors' Road* is not suitable for publication in the United States at the present time'.

Shortly afterwards Unwin Hyman wrote that they also had decided against proceeding with publication, adding the somewhat cryptic comment: 'It is a great pity that this fine book has missed the market.'

Preoccupied with problems of adjusting myself to routine journalism after four years writing almost exclusively about war, and with the unpleasant prospect of undergoing corrective surgery for a wound I had received in the Solomons, I did not ask for detailed reasons for the belated rejections.

Green Armour had been held up for six months by General Douglas MacArthur's censors because it was sharply critical of the training and equipment of both Australian and American troops committed to jungle warfare in the Pacific, so I assumed that some form of political pressure had been exerted on the publishers to discourage them from marketing another book which would irritate the military establishment by premature discussion of sensitive issues. *Conquerors' Road* dealt candidly with the behaviour of Allied troops in Germany, emphasised the alarming, grassroots hostility that existed between the Americans and Russians, questioned the wisdom of some military government policies, and expressed nonconformist views on German war guilt and the legitimacy of the Nuremberg trials of Nazis accused of major crimes against humanity.

By now well aware that truth is the first casualty in war and resigned to the realisation that victory over the Axis Powers had not brought peace to a world that was still bitterly divided on matters of political morality, I consigned the untimely manuscript to my collection of nonstarters, with the vague intention of digging it out and dusting it off when the passage of time had anaesthetised tender consciences.

As things were to turn out, I did not exhume and reread the text for nearly forty years — years in which a torrent of Second World War literature flooded from the printing presses. Official and unofficial histories, the memoirs, diaries and correspondence of statesmen and their advisers, service commanders and their aides, spymasters, propagandists and the inventors of nuclear weaponry, filled whole sections of reference libraries. Tales — sometimes fact, sometimes fiction or forgery — of high adventure, intrigue, brutality and treachery sold in millions all over the world.

Then, in the late 1960s and early 1970s, the flood subsided. Interest in books about the war in Europe was supplanted by interest in books about the conflict between East and West in Korea, South-East Asia and Indochina. However, when the embargo on public examination of classified documents in government archives was lifted after thirty years, a rich field of fresh source material became available to a new generation of historians; and the approach of the fortieth anniversary of the German surrender at Rheims encouraged publication of yet another spate of memoirs by those who, in one capacity or another, took part in the greatest blood-letting in human history.

Strangely enough, in all this vast accumulation of testimony about the execution of Hitler's Germany, the evidence of the spectator as distinct from the participant was seldom included.

When I resurrected the manuscript of *Conquerors' Road* and examined it with the kind of detachment that could only come from so long a preoccupation with different subject matter, I realised that it was a book written by a bystander who by choice looked out over the killing fields at ground level. It was straight reporting and straight commentary without benefit of hindsight — a contemporary chronicle by a licensed observer of a great triumph and a great tragedy.

Perhaps it throws some fresh light on the origins of the balance of terror which, political strategists claim, prevents the outbreak of a Third World War. Perhaps not.

That is for the reader to decide.

O. E. W.
Melbourne 1983

Germany, 1945
Photograph: Osmar White

Part I

THE WINTER OFFENSIVE

Chapter 1

The end began in winter, the hardest winter in memory on the German frontier. A shroud covered the whole land, snow four-and five-feet deep on level fields and the tops of the hedges drifted over. The great highways of north-western Europe were glazed with iron-hard ice and the wheeled traffic of war crawled over them perilously, clanking on chained tyres.

In January 1945, I went to Esch in Luxembourg, head-quarters of Patton's Third Army, to watch the slow gathering of men and machines and guns for the last offensive, the last massive leaning of American and British might against the ramparts of embattled Germany.

It was a dreary, sluggish war on the Ardennes Front now that von Rundstedt's sortie to Bastogne was finished; a war of snow-choked mountain forests, fought more to prise loose the clutch of winter than to finish the exhausted enemy. Waiting was hard on the strength and the spirit of the men, for the cold bit into their bones and blistered their skin and each one in his heart of hearts said, 'What is there to die for now? This time Hitler really must be beaten. Over those hills, down in that valley is Germany, getting the hell bombed out of it day after day and night after night. Pretty soon, when the frost lets up, we're going in to stay. How damned useless to die when there's no doubt who'll win!'

The road to liberation was almost travelled. The road of conquest lay ahead.

All the week a razor-edged wind blew snowclouds across the sky. The American line was on the western bank of the Our River, and the river was half-frozen. A battalion of the 4th Infantry Division was holding a ruined Luxembourish village near Dickirch. Field artillery was firing intermittently, battering the last of the Bastogne bulge flat against the ferroconcrete of the Siegfried Line. You could hear the shells go whooshing away over the pines and, long afterwards, the bump of the explosions among the German pillboxes. For an hour or so every morning and afternoon the enemy batteries replied, but the German gunners had no visual observation. Their fire fell erratically in the fields, sending up black spurts of steel and smoke and frozen earth. 'The krauts are through,' the battalion commander would say, watching the fall of shells. 'No sir, no ammunition, no men. It was over when we relieved Bastogne. Only this goddamn weather is holding us!'

The command post was in the cellar of a bakeshop, good and deep. One hadn't to worry, they said, even about the eighty-eights. The iron stove in the CP always glowed cherry-red, gorged with beams from the roof of the church, but rime still formed on the flap of canvas that hung over the cellar skylight. It was easy to understand why European armies fought so bitterly for the broken shells of what the Russians called 'inhabited places'. Even the dismal shelter of a cellar under a heap of fallen masonry was preferable to freezing in open fields and forests. The peril of shellfire in a town zeroed by enemy gunners was more endurable than the misery of existence with no shelter at all. While this weather lasted the limit of a soldier's endurance in the open was 24 hours.

At night, when snow fell and the wind fluted in the trees, you heard the men talk among themselves. Their talk was always talk of home, of the days that had been before the war and the days that might be after it — of women and liquor and privileged people. Seldom or never did they talk of why they were enduring their hardships. Long ago they had made the resolutions they needed. I thought about that, lying in the dark listening to the wind and the guns.

The second day up the line, the battalion commander said, 'You might as well stay on. Division's laid on a show over the river to clear some high ground that's worrying us. B and D companies will kick off in the morning. You could watch the start from an observation post near the D company's CP.'

I went forward at dawn with two company runners, riding in a jeep to the foot of the hill. 'You got plenty of time,' said the sergeant on the roadblock guard. 'Sorry we can't let you ride, but every time a jeep goes up the hill those poor suckers at the company CP get mortared. There's a stretch of road under observation, but the krauts never bother with one or two men going up on foot.'

With the first light a squadron of Mustangs bound on an interdiction mission passed overhead, just below the level of the broken clouds. They drew fire from enemy anti-aircraft batteries in the Siegfried Line. The bursts made dark blotches in the sky. Seconds later came the double thump of discharge and explosion. Far back of the line a section of 155 mm field guns started to fire. The cold bit face and hands and feet, and the snow squealed softly underfoot.

The road followed a spur onto the crest of the ridge. There had been fighting for this high ground too. The snow had not smoothed away the shape of the shell-holes in the fields. Here and there along the ditches were sticks thrust into buried mounds, on each stick a steel helmet. Behind the crest was a group of stone farm buildings and beyond that a village with its roofs blown off and gaps torn in the walls.

The runners fell into single file and veered off the road towards the farm buildings. 'Keep on the trail, bud,' they said. 'We only moved in here last night and the shoulders ain't been deloused yet.'

There was a dead cow in the barn. She lay on her back, legs stiffly thrust up and udder distended. Round the corner of the barn was a dead Tiger tank, with a charred corpse half through its turret hatch. You could still smell burning.

The CP was in the farmhouse cellar, down a flight of ten stone steps. The room was crowded with men sitting on army cots by the light of a gasoline lantern. A signals corporal operated his portable switchboard by the light of two candles set in the necks of schnapps bottles.

'Whee-ee!' somebody said, 'look what's arrived — the press!' The company commander shook hands.

'Pardon the glove,' he said grinning, 'I've a touch of frost... Can I see your identification?...' Then, 'Pipe down, fellas, it's only the Limey press.'

There was a concerted groan.

'We're just finished briefing. Oh, they briefed you at battalion? Come up to watch the show? Well, there's a good story out of last night, anyway. Anybody here who was on that deal last night?'

'I was, sir.'

'Where's Stowski?'

'Don't know, sir.'

'Well, it doesn't matter. It was like this. We had a patrol out, spotting the krauts' foxholes for today, see? Six men and Sergeant Stowski. Stowski was out on his belly in front of the others when the krauts fired a flare. He was only twelve feet from a machine-gun pit and they saw him and opened up. They didn't hit him, but he was pinned down.'

The corporal's telephone whirred. 'Captain Engels... yes, sir.'

The company commander reached out, snatched the phone and said, 'Hullo, hullo, hullo. Who's this? Who?... Oh, yes. Yes, that's right. They have, have they? Who? Oh. Do they know what sort of chance he has? I see. Well, that's one damned good man we've lost...one damned good man.' His voice and his face in the lantern light were quite expressionless. 'Listen,' he went on, into the phone, 'I want a working party of four men up to bury a dead kraut as soon as we move off. He's stuck half-in and half-out of that truck we knocked out last night. He's pretty burned up, so they better bring a couple of blankets or some canvas. Okay. Yes, I will.'

He seemed to have forgotten about Stowski's good story. He took a message pad and sat down and started writing in it.

I went over to the man who said he had been with Stowski, sat down on the cot beside him, and said: 'Tell me about the patrol. It sounds like a good story.'

Just as he started to reply there was a thin, high whistle followed by a crash. The lights flickered and the blanket over the cellar door stirred.

'They're early,' someone said, then to me: 'You cut it a bit fine, didn't you? Eighty-eights this morning, too. Well!'

Ten seconds later there was another crash, and the company commander said: 'Heavy mortar. Maybe you fellas had better move away from the door.'

The bombardment lasted twelve minutes. Eighty-seven rounds of mortar and 88 mm shells. Most of them fell in the streets of the village, but the overs were near enough to rock the cellar walls.

The man who had been with Stowski persistently told me the story — in considerable detail which I do not remember. But the gist of it was that the sergeant had been pinned down for six hours with the Germans firing bursts over him. He foxed dead. He didn't blink. At three o'clock in the morning a German climbed out the gun pit, crawled over, kicked him and took off his overshoes. Still he didn't even blink. Half an hour later another German crawled out and took his billfold. It was true, no kidding. In the morning Stowski didn't have his overshoes or his billfold...

When the shelling stopped, the telephone buzzed again and the company commander said: 'No, no,' several times. Then: 'Okay, we'd appreciate that.'

After the gloom of the cellar the snow light was blinding. Four men came from the smoking village at a jogtrot. They wore white caps and hoods cobbled up from sheets and table linen taken from farmhouses, but these were stained with yellow earth. The steam spurted from their mouths as they panted along.

'They got Stowski,' the leader said as he passed. 'Buried him with a mortar burst. He's hurt pretty bad.'

'Christ,' said the man beside me. 'What lousy luck!'

The observation post was in a belt of fir trees. It overlooked the river meadows and stands of young timber running down to them. From there one could clearly mark the fall of the shells on the hill opposite. Before the two companies assigned to the attack moved through their outpost positions there was half an hour of intensive artillery preparation. The river was three hundred feet below, running only in a narrow course between margins of ice.

The beginning of the attack was invisible. When it had been going twenty minutes, some machine-guns opened up and the sound echoed and re-echoed in the valley, more sharply than the heavier tone of cannon. For the first time figures could be seen moving over the white fields. Half-a-dozen men tramped stolidly through the drifts directly below the observation post, set up a machine-gun near a clump of willows and began firing it. By now clouds of dust and smoke were rising from a target concealed by trees and a fold in the land, the German counterpart of the ruined village near the company CP. The barrage had grown really heavy.

'Ten shells for their one,' said the man who had been detailed to show me the sights. 'That's the secret of it. That shifts them. You won't see anything more now, sir. Let's get going.'

The invisible manoeuvres in the valley and the barrage had loosened the German defence. Behind us a line of weapon carriers was coming up the road, interspersed with command jeeps. There was no enemy fire.

Troops awaiting orders to go forward were prying into the village cellars again looking for schnapps. Signallers were already running out wire from big, black reels, looping it on the bare hedgerows.

I went down the hill on foot, keeping as close as I could to fresh vehicle tracks for fear of mines. The sun came out for a while and the winter morning sparkled. There was steam over the river. The engineers had already built a footbridge in a good concealed spot between willow clumps on which long icicles were hanging. A section of men was guarding it, squatting dejectedly near their cover. They were wet and unshaven and red-eyed. They regarded me without curiosity.

I went across the bridge, looking down at the ice and the shallow green water with long waving strands of weeds. Machine-gun fire had killed one of the engineers who built the bridge and it was yet too soon to have recovered his body. He lay, his clothing caught on a snag, in among the weeds, staring up at the sky.

On the far side of the bridge the church spire of the German village was visible, but a few yards along the road I met the lieutenant who had been with the company commander in the farm cellar. He was hurrying, excited, and in a bad temper.

'You scram outta here,' he said. 'You got your dateline. You've been in Germany. They're forming up for a counter-attack now. They'd counterattack with five blind men on crutches, the mad bastards! You scram outta here! There's an SP gun up the road.'

So I scrammed out of Germany, over the footbridge, past the dead engineer, up the hill and into the farmhouse cellar. But only the signals corporal and a private were left, whirling their telephone handles. A thickening procession of transport was on the road.

Patton's army was advancing into the Rhineland on the road to Bitburg and the Kyll.

Chapter 2

Another bridge led into Germany over the Sauer River at Echternach. It was built of raw lumber on the remains of a stone arch that had withstood the violence of centuries until one morning American tanks nosed through the rubble of the town and a German sapper, peering though the embrasures of a pillbox on the ridge opposite, moved his hand to signal the demolition. A second man pressed down the handles of a plunger. The old arch heaved and fell down into the hurrying water.

When the new bridge was built in early March they nailed up a notice on it the first day: 'YOU ARE NOW ENTERING GERMANY — NO FRATERNISING!'

The Army newspaper, *Stars and Stripes*, recorded that the Russians posted their entry into Germany differently. Their signpost read: 'THE LAIR OF THE BEAST'.

I used to ponder the difference.

The big push was on. For hundreds of miles to the rear the roads, now thawed and rainswept, were crowded with transport bringing up men and equipment for the last great heave.

This traffic moved for the most part very slowly, and was unevenly spaced. There were mud-smothered tanks, tank-destroyers and half-tracks; armoured troop vehicles, jeeps, trucks, tank-wagons, staff cars; crazy-looking amphibious craft, weasels, ducks; pontoons, boats, floats on their carriers;

tarpaulined guns and limbers, cranes, piledrivers, hoists, bulldozers, graders, scoops and rollers. They all snorted and roared and crashed along nose to tail, weaving out of one another's columns on the long, straight poplar-fringed roads.

Great dumps of gasoline in jerry cans grew up by crossroads. Behind the ditches of every byroad lay ranks of artillery ammunition in hexagonal wooden cases painted brown or green. Rows of howitzer shells thrust their snouts out of the springing grass and brush.

The sky was full of friendly aircraft all day long. They scurried low over the treetops, or up behind the clouds. The noise they made was like the noise of a gargantuan beehive. When they came down on the enemy, the ripping sound of their guns echoed in the orchards, along the courses of winding brooks and in the forests. Sometimes there was a muffled rumble of bombs.

This was happening all the way from the North Sea to the Alps.

I watched the faces of the men riding the tanks and trucks, holding themselves stiff against the shudder and lurch of skids on the muddy pave. Did they, too, take time out to reflect that this was happening all the way from the North Sea to the Alps; or to wonder why and by what process of global effort it was happening?

It was hard to see the fighting in this preliminary stage of the last offensive. One went forward and heard guns firing at German vehicle concentrations and dug-in troops; or perhaps saw, head lifted fearfully above the line of a ditch or stone wall, shellbursts a mile away, or the walls of a fortified house crumbling behind the gauze of smoke.

Yet here and there the Germans put up a stubborn resistance and counterattacked. Men wounded in these encounters, sitting dazed with shock at the clearing stations, told tales of hand-to-hand fighting and the long ecstatic agony of serving machine-guns with sights on living targets. They told of fights in stark mountain woods with ice-cold rain falling; of fording waist-deep rivers; of tanks bellowing down roads, spurting tracer; or prisoners rumoured to have been murdered in cold blood.

'Those krauts are mad,' a little, yellow-faced Charleston sergeant told me, staring at the streaks of dried blood on the backs of his hands. 'Y'see, we heard them up the road first. They ran over our foxholes with grenades and then started firing green flares for their tanks. Our gun got thirty or more, just like that. But they was SS. They kept coming. They didn't even have the sense to keep their heads down. Goddamn! Then their burp-guns started to open up back of where our company headquarters was, and we got the hell out of it. Lindner and Sands never made it — just this guy here and me. You never saw such a f-----g snafu!'

He shivered and put his hands into his pockets.

At headquarters the briefing officers dismissed such affairs in a couple of dozen offhand words: 'The enemy counterattacked before dawn with about two hundred infantry, four tanks and two self-propelled guns. Our outposts withdrew a few hundred yards, but by nightfall the position had been restored.'

The morning of 6 March was chilly. There was high cloud over the Sauer Valley, but rain was falling only in the highlands to the east.

Folds of treeless ridges rose up on the German side of the river. Perhaps, once upon a time, this country had been beautiful in a quiet, broad, pastoral sort of way. But not now. It was dirty, grimed all over with waiting for battle, and the battle itself. Reddish-yellow dust powdered the neglected fields which had not known plough or harrow for years. They were empty fields. No beasts grazed in them. There were no birds in the hedgerows. The pasture was covered with slivers of tarnished foil showered from high-flying aeroplanes to confuse the German radar. The thin metal reflected the radiation of detection stations and deceived screen-watchers trying to assess the numbers and course of approaching aircraft.

The road, I realised suddenly, was running through the Siegfried Line. Quadruple rows of 'dragons' teeth' flanked the macadam and curved away out of sight, following the contours of the ridges. Each tooth was a firmly anchored obelisk of concrete about four-feet high. The teeth were set close to one another. The defence was far less spectacular than dramatically angled cameras would have had the world believe. It looked trifling, piddling — more like a fence built by a rich eccentric than the trumpeted apron of Hitler's west wall.

All modern fortifications are unspectacular. It is part of their science that they should be. Even the great, useless casemates of the Maginot Line looked from the outside — and smelt from the inside — more like sewerage works than subterranean forts.

Except for the anticlimactic dragons' teeth, the Siegfried Line was very nearly invisible from the roads which passed through it. Only by staring and by knowing from experience where to stare could one see the long, blackened slits through which the muzzles of antitank and machine-guns had once been thrust. Each slit commanded a section of countryside interlocked with the next and the next, so that in theory every conceivable approach to the Rhineland could be raked by lead. But it never worked that way in practice. When the German armies fell back on the Line they no longer had the troops to man every fortification, nor enough ammunition for every gun. The Allied artillery found out the forts one by one. Armour-piercing shells and rockets gnawed blue gashes in the concrete out of which the rubble filling poured. A line of such forts, three hundred miles long, was made untenable by saturation bombardment or by bazooka-men and tanks armed with nozzles to squirt sixty-foot jets of flaming oil into the loopholes.

Each abandoned pillbox was now no more than a death pit blackened with fire and high explosive. I never actually saw one of these fortifications cleared by flamethrowers, but men who did told me that when the tanks closed in the Germans either came out screaming for mercy; or, if they stayed, stayed silent and were taken out by burial squads with shovels and tarpaulins.

By the time I saw them, the pillboxes were cold, blackened, cluttered with horrible rubbish — and the charred and twisted mementos of human beings. They stank of burnt flesh.

Here and there the roads to the Sauer passed farmhouses, or what had been farmhouses: stone heaps surrounding cellars. Since Hitler came into power those houses had been rebuilt with thick, loopholed walls for defence. What sort of farmers had lived in them? What sort of women were their wives? What sort of children were their children? Did these families feel afraid because their houses had been turned into forts on a disputed frontier? Did they see the connection between the embrasures that served them for windows and the growing barrenness of their fields?

The belt of devastation, of complete and lifeless quiet between the grid of teeming roads that carried the forces of the invasion, extended from the frontier to a depth of about thirty kilometres. Beyond that, the violence of the battle had diminished. The coherence of the German defence had begun to break up when the zone of fixed fortifications was pierced.

The nature of the country began to change. Forests of young pines and oaks came struggling down into the fields. Here it was raining. I was almost startled to see a horse cropping grass in a field, and two ducks swimming in a muddy pond near a farmhouse that had not been demolished.

There had, however, been sporadic fighting in the woods. Aircraft and artillery had caught concentrations of guns and vehicles in clearings or along firebreaks and sideroads. There were camouflaged trucks and vans with green boughs of pine still heaped over them, long-nosed eighty-eights pitched over on one wheel with their breechblocks missing or smashed. There were heaps of picked-over clothing, rifles, torn books, records, technical equipment, hasty new graves — the leavings of a broken army.

The first prisoners taken beyond the Kyll River were coming to the rear, jammed thirty or forty men in a truck. Except for their shapeless grey-green uniforms they looked very much the same sort of human beings as the American infantry, jammed thirty or forty men in a truck, moving up. Their faces had the same expression of resignation and inward brooding. The only difference was that one seldom saw them smile.

A few miles farther on, gangs of prisoners were employed breaking stones to fill the crumbling shoulders of the road, or shovelling into the ditches the greyish slush collecting on the tarmac. Most of these men were either younger or older than soldiers ought to be. They looked docile, sunk in misery. They clawed at the broken stone with their red hands, or swung the heavy sledges slowly, or shovelled the mud with imperceptible result. Their guards were bored and cold. Now and then one warmed himself by cursing a slow or sick worker, yelling: Get along there you ----sucking sonofabitch! Pick 'em up! Get going!'

From one gang, two SS men had tried to escape into the forest. The guards had shot them. Their bodies had rolled over and over in the muddy grass. Their uniforms and the skin of their faces and hands were coated evenly with a fine layer of slime. They looked like overturned statues. Beyond them the long, tarred road stretched straight on into Germany, shining in the drizzle.

Enemy territory. In the early days of the advance there was always disquiet in the thought that henceforward the war was invasion of Germany. I used to ask soldiers, now and then, did they feel sort of queer walking about in Germany. Mostly they admitted they did, usually under the camouflage of tough talk: 'Well, the ----s had it coming to them. They could have stayed and rotted in the goddamn country till the end of their days if they hadn't moved out and tried to kick the whole world about!' But yes. It *was* sort of queer, walking about in Germany.

Ruins like Bitburg, or Jülich or Düren, gave the men a sort of wooden-faced exultation. You could feel them think, 'This is the pay-off.'

But those ruins were deserted except for the dead. It wasn't quite so simple when the war burst through into country from which all the civilians had not been evacuated.

A few miles north of Bitburg a village was cut off before its inhabitants could flee. It was an ugly place — a mean, jammed-together collection of stone houses inhabited by ugly people. In Europe you find villages where, it seems, the whole population is ill-favoured. There had been a brisk small-arms and mortar fight here before the battle passed on. Roofs were holed and walls torn away, but the place was still habitable. The streets were rivers of reddish mud flowing round the carcasses of horses and cattle.

A command post had been set up in the church for a few hours, but the soldiers had gone. Swarms of yellow-haired children scampered indoors from the path of our jeep. The villagers crowded to the doorways and windows to watch us pass — stunned and slackjawed, yet unable to resist the temptation of novelty. I remember particularly the face of one sixteen-year-old girl with pale, protruding blue eyes and a full, loose mouth. She wore her hair in pigtails and plastered her snub nose against an unbroken windowpane. As the jeep backed to negotiate a sharp turn in the street, her eyes met mine unwinkingly. The whole loose, blonde face contracted into a scowl in which fear, bewilderment and hate of the foreigner were blended.

An old farmer leaning on a stick pressed his body back against a closed door.

'*Kommen Sie hier!*' — the conquerors' unfailing formula. Come here.

He shuffled two paces forward and snatched at his hat.

'Where are the American soldiers?'

'They are gone. They went yesterday.'

'When was the fighting here?'

'There was fighting here today — in the early hours, before dawn.'

'Now tell the truth — how many German soldiers are in the village?'

'None. They all went away.'

'Tell the truth. It will be bad for this village if you do not tell the truth.'

'I am telling the truth.'

'So. Why are the people still in this village?'

'There was not time for them to go away before the Americans came.'

'Did the people wish to go?'

The old man shrugged. 'The people had no choice. They were ordered to go, but there was no way of going.'

'Is there any food in the village?'

'No. Only what the people have in their cellars.'

'Is that the truth?'

'Yes.'

'Are you afraid of the American soldiers?'

He looked at me quite blankly. Then he said: 'Germany is finished. Hitler is finished.'

I wanted to talk to him, my first German civilian on his own doorstep, but there was no point of contact between his mind and mine. Words came stiffly. It was foolish to have spoken to him in the first place. 'Okay,' I said to the driver, 'let's go!'

He revved, let in the clutch. The wheels raced for a second, throwing up a sheet of slush which struck the old man at the level of the knees, drenching him. He stood with his hat in his hand looking after us.

The driver hunched over the wheel, wrenching it savagely this way and that to keep out of ruts.

'Jesus,' he said, 'what a place! What a goddamn place!'

The 5th Infantry Division was piling through in any sort of order to consolidate the ground taken by the 4th Armored beyond the Kyll. There was always a good deal of confusion about what ground had been cleared of the enemy and what hadn't. Forward of the infantry columns there were long stretches of deserted road where the going was always tense.

All the towns were more or less beaten up by the tanks. Some of them still burned. Travellers in the rear of the armoured columns passed through them as hastily as might be.

But in one such town west of Mayen, twenty or thirty American soldiers and a dozen trucks were dispersed about the central square. They told us there was a long stretch of road with no cover ahead. A few kraut aircraft were sneaking in under the cloud cover, strafing. It would be better to wait a while.

The town's inhabitants were clearing possessions out of the wrecked houses, women and children trundling handcarts and perambulators piled high with clothing and pots and pans. It was hard to understand just what they were doing.

'*Kommen Sie hier*. Where are you going?'

'I am going to my sister's house.'

'Why?'

'A shell came through the roof of our house and the water pipes burst...'

'*Kommen Sie hier*. Where are you going?'

'To my father's house.'

'Where?'

'In the Ruppertstrasse.'

'What number?'

'Seventeen.'

'Why are you going?'

'My mother has been killed. I am going to keep house for my father. It is better for a family to be together in such times. Is it permitted? It is not forbidden?'

'No. It is not forbidden as far as I know.'

Rain kept falling spasmodically.

The convent schoolhouse was in the square. Half-a-dozen nuns were busily herding young children about. They were organising a dormitory for them in the basement — belatedly.

Some of the children escaped the shepherding and were standing about the trucks. Others were playing subdued hopscotch on the pavement.

One boy of about twelve years wearing a Hitler jugend cap with the badge taken off kept staring at me, grinning.

'*Kommen Sie hier*. You. What is your name?'

'Manfred.'

'Where are your father and mother?'

'My mother is in Berlin. My father is in the Wehrmacht, fighting.'

He was still grinning.

'Why are you smiling?'

The grin flickered uncertainly.

'You have a funny uniform,' he said. 'Are you English?'

'Yes. But never mind that. Why are you wearing that cap?'

'All the boys wear this cap.'

'It is a Hitler Youth cap, isn't it?'

'No. All the boys wear it.'

'Don't lie to me. I am not ignorant. It is a Hitler Youth cap.'

His eyes dropped.

'The *Herr* says so.'

'Do you love the Führer?'

'No.'

'Why? Why don't you love the Führer?'

'Germany is finished.'

'Did you ever love the Führer?'

'No.'

'*Never*?'

'No.'

'You are a dreadful liar, aren't you? Did not all German children love the Führer?'

'The *Herr* says so.'

'Run away, then.'

He backed off.

Was he trained and prompted to lying — fostering the thought: 'You poor fool foreigner. Little do you know what the Führer has in store for you?' It was impossible to tell.

A half an hour later, four or five German fighter bombers flew over the town at low altitude and circled back. They fired a few bursts. Twenty millimetre cannon mounted on the trucks and the flak waggons of a convoy down the road opened up in reply. A hail of steel whistled over the rooftops.

The children screamed and rushed for the schoolhouse. A coifed nun, her mouth open soundlessly in her pasty face, stood in the door giving them ineffectual little shoves towards the cellar stairs.

I bent double and bolted for cover. A fat woman darted in front of me, panting and shrieking thinly, clawing at the children.

One of the truckmen was standing in the schoolhouse hall cursing. A bomb whistled. I dropped on one knee and put my head up against the stone staircase. The flags of the floor leapt up and rocked and dust fell. The cannon spat twice as hard.

A second bomb dropped farther off. Then the firing began to diminish. Up the cellar stairs came the sound of the nuns and the children praying and sobbing.

The truckman set his helmet straight, spat on the floor, and said deliberately: 'Shit!' The firing stopped. He went to the door and looked out.

There was hardly a minute of silence before children started to come outdoors again. Farther down the street was a hospital. It had a Red Cross flag hanging on the fence and two large crosses painted on the roof. A flight of steps led up to the entrance. A nurse in striped uniform and starched cap waddled down carrying a bucketful of water which she sloshed over the bottom steps to wash off muddy footprints. She turned and waddled up again.

Opposite the schoolhouse, a lane led into the square. A young woman in a tweed suit emerged from it and stood looking around. One of the children, a small boy with brown stockings pulled up over his knees, ran across to her. She caught him up in her arms. For a moment, his thin brown legs seemed to dangle out of her belly. Then she put him down gently and together they went off up the lane.

The children resumed their hopscotch game, scuffling over the pavement.

That night we reached Polch, but the CP of the armoured column had already moved on, leaving only a rear echelon to direct supply. One part of the town had been cleared of civilians to provide billets for incoming troops.

We ate supper — a supply miracle of chicken, peas, potatoes and canned peaches — in the local inn, washing the food down with thin, sweet ale out of the beer engines.

'The civilians? No trouble — no trouble at all,' they told me. 'There won't be yet a while. We're moving too fast. The krauts don't know what's hit 'em...'

But the sentries in the streets were jumpy.

It was a very dark night, very still. To the north and east flickers of bluish light ran along the skyline where guns were firing and the searchlights beyond the Rhine were seeking out aircraft.

Whoever had lived in my billet, a four-floored house of stuccoed stone, had been reasonably prosperous. It was very clean. It smelled of *Waschpulver* and wax polish. The best parlour was not a room which had been lived in. Its oak furniture was stiffly ranged along the walls. An oval photograph of an old man with Kaiser moustaches stared arrogantly down from the mantel. There were Dresden plates and pewter steins and antlers, a leadlighted bookcase with leatherbound sets of Goethe and Schiller and some anthologies of poetry. The soldiers assigned billets here did not brave the forbidding primness of that room. They crowded together for company about a tiled stove in a sitting room next to the kitchen, drank nips of looted brandy and told dirty stories.

In the kitchen was a large electric range, and a dresser full of good china. There was a cupboard stocked with brown flour, beans, pots of jam, crackers and patent medicines; a cellar full of onions and potatoes and kegs of new wine. In the back of the linen closet, was a jar half-full of hard candy.

'The sonofabitches,' my driver said softly, 'they didn't go without much, did they? All that cock about Germany starving.'

On the floors above were the bedrooms and more store cupboards. The wardrobes were full of clothing. It was an amusing game trying to deduce how many people have lived there — and what kind of people. Three or four children, obviously. Two young women and an older woman, one man, or perhaps two.

From letters in a desk drawer, I discovered that the head of the household was a dentist. Photographs and field-service cards indicated that he had two sons fighting, one an officer.

The wife was evidently thrifty. Her linen cupboards were full and the old linen was beautifully patched and mended. Her thrift would probably have been irritating to live with. She hoarded. She had drawers full of odd buttons and patches and tins and broken furniture fittings. Somebody in the family had once sold quick-dye preparations for use in the house. There were piles of advertising pamphlets and cartons of samples in a chest. The women had between them five evening frocks and a little store of French cosmetics... The older woman was a devout Catholic. Her dresser drawers were full of Christopher medals, prayerbooks, strings of rosary beads. Over her bed was a singularly horrible wooden crucifix. The dentist collected pipes...

Ordinary people, these. One felt a vague stirring of shame, prying into their drawers, ferreting out their trivial domestic secrets...

In the man's tallboy was a collection of tax receipts and demands for contributions to patriotic funds; apologetic letters from a Frankfurt dentists' supply house explaining the wartime shortage of materials.

Yes, very ordinary people. Yet not quite. In the attic, where items of the family washing still hung drying, was a wooden carpenter's tool chest. Under layers of Berlin picture papers was concealed a collection of magnificently produced Nazi propaganda books, and a bundle of photographs of the family at local party rallies. They had evidently been hidden there on the approach of the enemy. There had not been time to destroy them.

It was a rather sickening discovery. I had felt a growing friendliness — a growing tolerance, at least — for this unknown family in whose home I sheltered.

The attic windows were unshuttered. One could see up and down the street, and over the lower part of the town. It was dark and silent. No lights blinked. Where were the women and the children and Nazi dentist? Gunflashes kept running up and down the skyline. It was chilly and a gust of drizzle blew in.

It was not hard to project one's mind on the wings of the night — northward to Godesburg, Bonn, Cologne, Krefeld, Goch and Cleves. There, behind the veil of darkness, the armies of conquest were thrusting deeper and deeper. A dark, secretly moving force with long proboscises thrust out ahead of it, splitting, dividing, disintegrating the land of the enemy, each proboscis tipped by a twinkle of fire...

Land of the enemy. Land of...what? Of Nazi dentists and old men leaning on sticks, snatching at their hats? Or housewives who hoarded buttons and hid candy from the children in the linen closet? Land of children playing hopscotch, of praying nuns, and waddling nurses? Land of men in grey-green uniforms with red hands fumbling stones? Land of *liebst du den Führer*? Land and lair of the beast?

All these...

During the night, the sound of a great force of bombers awakened me. They passed for more than two hours, drumming against the silence of the fallen town. I dreamed uneasily, of a city burning and men in little, tilted, padded seats watching — not the burning city — but the green glow of their instrument boards.

Chapter 3

We caught up with the tanks of the 4th Division at Besignheim. Combat Command B had set up its CP in the local castle. Steel tracks had ploughed up the sodden turf of the park. A Sherman had skidded and demolished a section of its ancient, vine-covered stone wall. The archway by the lodge was chipped and scraped by steel. The castle had ramparts and high mullioned windows. Its rooms were of noble size with polished parquetry floors and elaborately moulded ceilings. On the walls were gloomy paintings in heavy gilt frames — hideous, and no doubt very valuable.

A man in a black coat and high starched collar sat at an escritoire in the great hall, busily writing lists on sheets of foolscap paper. His hair was clipped scalp-tight. Folds of pink, fat neck bulged over the collar. A pair of gold-rimmed pince-nez sat on his nose. He looked too German to be quite true.

I asked a young lieutenant standing outside the G2's door, 'What the hell's he doing?'

'Making up lists of requisitioned articles,' the lieutenant replied dryly. 'He's working on an inventory. We just let him alone. He's happy. He's out of mischief. Have you seen the baroness yet? Nope? Well, you should. Quite something, quite something. But the skipper fixed her. You ought to interview her at the village inn. Quite something.'

The skipper was friendly.

'Sure, take a look up front. You're welcome,' he said. 'We got a patrol of light tanks going out in about an hour'... He turned to the map. 'We want to take a look at three villages — down here along the river. We want to see if we can draw fire from the other bank. That's the idea of a light tank patrol, you know. Draw fire and get a fix on the gun positions.'

He spoke very cheerfully. I said with some misgiving that I would report back in an hour. I went down and watched a battery of field artillery move into a water meadow behind the castle, align the guns, and start to lob shells in the direction of Coblenz. Then I went down and saw the baroness — a blonde woman about twenty-five years old, with a pale, sharp-featured face. She wore breeches and high, polished boots, a tweed coat and a checked stock fastened with a silver brooch. She carried a riding crop. A defence against impertinent soldiery? The soldiery lounged about chewing gum and eyeing her with interest only faintly disguised under sardonic half-grins.

The baroness said she had been living quietly for two years, here at the family seat in Besignheim. Her husband had been killed on the Eastern Front. Neither he nor she had been members of the Party. She had taken no interest in politics before the war. She had heard the air-raid damage was very great in Berlin, but she had not been in the capital since 1941. She had been looking after evacuated children and convalescent soldiers at the castle here.

A lifeless, non-committal story...

When I got back to the castle the tanks were forming up. The skipper came out and I heard him telling someone by radiophone that he was sending a squadron to look over coordinates such and such, and such and such; and there was a correspondent going up the line. Then he said to the patrol leader: 'Look, there's no great hurry — let the press have a look at what our TDs did to that column down the next village.'

I climbed into the spare driver's seat. The driver had four days' beard and chewed tobacco stolidly.

'Keep your finger off them tits, bud,' he said, 'unless you need to. She's charged. If they open up with small stuff, then duck your seat and close the hatch. If it's big stuff it don't matter. These goddamn things ain't got any armour anyway. But at least we can move, and that's sumpin'. Give me the "lights" any day.'

The engines came to life. The column formed up and filed down the main street, the population scuttling out of the way.

Beyond the town the road ran straight and narrow through plum and apple orchards where the first blossoms were swelling on the gnarled trees. Spring promised to come early. The fields were smooth with centuries of cultivation. A steady drizzle was falling out of the overcast sky. Moss blotted the tree-trunks and the crumbling stone walls. The tank squadron was strung out at fifty-yard intervals.

We turned off the road and ran down a gentle hill towards a village with its roofs and chimneys showing above a young plantation. The driver leaned over, yelled something and pointed. I jumped. He grinned and shook his head. It was only a wrecked waggon he was pointing out.

Then there were more wrecked waggons. This was the beginning of a two-mile stretch of slaughter. The remnants of three or four Wehrmacht divisions had fled this way from the Kyll — without coordination of any kind. They were headed for the Kronprinz Wilhelm Bridge across the Rhine. Fast-moving American armour was on their heels. Shellfire knocked out their leading vehicles in a narrow street and a great traffic jam piled up. Up and down the doomed column the gunners ranged their fire, blowing to pieces more than three hundred trucks and cars, two hundred horse-drawn waggons and scores of field pieces and anti-aircraft guns.

The charred wreckage grew thicker in the ditches. Twisted metal was mixed with fragmented carcasses of horses, and human remains. Blood stained the rain puddles crimson. A flattened corpse lay in the centre of the roadway and the tanks passed over it.

We came into the half-burned town. Children were running in and out of the wreckage. The eyes of the grown-ups were heavy, almost indifferent. They took no notice of the bodies lying in the gutters. Yet to look hard at them was to get some gesture of submission — a nervously touched hat, a half-smile. From the windows of every house hung a white flag on a pole or a broomstick.

Farther on we came to villages not yet officially surrendered, but there was no resistance. On the roadblock before the entrance of one of them, Saint Sebastian, some defiant patriot had daubed the English words 'See Germany and Die!' But inside the roadblock the white flags hung out just the same. The men tipped their hats, the women ran indoors to warn any wounded stragglers they might be hiding, 'American tanks! American tanks!'

Only once did I see a gesture of hostility, and that was pitiful. An old man in dark clothes came out of a sidestreet, hurrying. He looked like a schoolmaster. He had to jump to escape getting hit. His red face paled. His testy mouth twisted and his eyes sparkled with hate. I saw his fists clench as he turned away and stamped off over the cobbles, twitching with unspoken curses on the invader.

On the farther outskirts of the same village we came on a house where the family was eating dinner. At the sound of the tank engines two young children came rushing on to the porch. Their bibs were still round their necks. They stood on the top step with their hands held stiffly up in surrender. It was too much for the commander of the tank ahead. He waved them sharply to put their hands down. The children's faces split into timid smiles. The last I saw of them, their hands were still raised, but they were now waving frantically.

A jingle ran in my head. The last line: 'And who shall wash the river Rhine? ...'

The river here was three hundred yards wide. The far bank rose sheer into a range of hills which, unlike this rustic western bank, was populous with clusters of brick and stone warehouses, factories and dwellings. One could see spires of churches, the fat fingers of factory chimneys and behind them high up on a hill, the battlements of a round tower built maybe a thousand years ago.

The column halted. The commanders stood up in their turrets studying the east bank. The world was still. Ahead, Coblenz was burning, columns of smoke rising from its ruins.

Barges and tugs, still and deserted, were anchored in long lines at the river quays. There was no sign of life, but something was moving — the green, smooth river itself, hurrying on. Then, far away on the hazy hills a sullen red flash showed out and a shell whistled over and thumped in a field.

'Okay? Got it?' The man in the turret of the leading tank waved a clenched fist in circles. The engines roared very loud as we wheeled off the road and the skyline cut long curved gashes behind us in the orchard turf.

Later that day we questioned prisoners in a cage on the road back to Polch. The account of one thin Wehrmacht sergeant, who claimed to have been a lecturer in physics at Bonn University, was concise and credible. Wehrmacht units assigned to defend strongpoints in the Rhineland, he said, had specific orders not to retreat. They were to defend their positions to the death. In the early part of the breakthrough many units were determined to obey this order, but when supply broke down men found they couldn't be heroes with empty stomachs and empty ammunition cases. The only troops permitted to retreat were the seriously wounded. The slightly wounded and sick were sent back to the line again and again. Every battle ended the same way. A position would be surrounded but the Americans never closed in to reduce it. They simply pounded it out of existence with artillery. When officers found survivors who had broken through the encirclement they ordered them to report to a collection point. There, irrespective of age, condition or training, they were assigned to a new position and told to be sure to carry out their orders this time — hold it or die.

There were very few unwounded Wehrmacht officers left, the sergeant went on. Sometimes corporals were in command of the remnants of battalions. When they were sent to a new position, they were promised tank or artillery support, but the support never materialised, and the whole business of encirclement, saturation, and fragmentary escape started all over again.

I asked what section of the army exercised sufficient control to force beaten and exhausted men into such a cycle. The SS, the sergeant replied. The SS were running everything now. The SS were the army.

Was there no move to mutiny? Wouldn't it be better to disobey and live to fight another day? The sergeant shrugged. What's the difference between getting killed by the SS man and getting killed by the Americans? Look what happened on the Kronprinz Wilhelm Bridge... Only SS units were permitted to retreat across the river. When the tanks and guns caught the traffic block some hundreds of men escaped into the fields.

At daylight, a group of fifty or sixty went across the bridge. There was some firing on the other side but nobody knew why. A mob of two or three hundred then started to cross. When the leaders were halfway across, the demolition charges set by the engineers under the bridge pylons were fired. The main span collapsed and scores of fugitives were thrown into the river or crushed in the collapsing web of steel. Machine-guns on the far bank then opened fire on swimmers.

This, said the ex-lecturer of Bonn University, was the SS way of doing things. There could be no revolt against it, but Germany was finished. No flesh and blood — even German flesh and blood driven by the SS — could stand up against so many guns, so many tanks.

'It is a world in which might is right, eh, sergeant?'

He looked at me for a moment, not quite following my bad German. Then one corner of his mouth twitched slightly.

British troops in Germany, 1945
Photograph: Osmar White

Part II

SPRINGTIME IN GERMANY

Chapter 4

Through March and the first half of April the invasion of western Germany moved so fast that, even in retrospect, the pace of the campaign seems unreal.

After the Ardennes counteroffensive had failed in December, Germany's military position was hopeless. Yet resistance continued because the German Army and the German people, though exhausted, still reacted automatically to the discipline of the police state.

This unreasoned resistance cost the country dearly. When the Allied armies moved to deliver the death blow they moved with enormous strength. The Canadian divisions driving south from Holland through Cleves to link up with the First and Ninth US armies in the centre were the only troops who encountered forces strong enough to offer real battle. Elsewhere there was fighting — fighting of varying intensity — but no more.

After the Siegfried Line was breached, the advance to the Rhine was a manoeuvre against resistance only strong enough to justify the demolition of town after town and village after village by shellfire to save casualties. Thousands of aeroplanes were dispatched to pulverise again the gutted Rhineland cities and to slaughter convoys of fugitives struggling to reach and cross the river.

This execution was to continue until May: to continue until the whole of Germany, with the exception of south-eastern Bavaria, was mauled beyond belief.

After the breakthroughs in early March there were no more 'lines'. The tank columns moved almost at will and at a speed calculated to prevent the enemy ever re-establishing coherent defence. The problem for commanders was not to force a way through enemy positions but to maintain supply and communication while their steel cavalry carved the country into pieces.

A column of armour would approach a village or town and deploy in cover. A tank or half-track, known as the 'bulsh waggon' and fitted with large amplifiers, would be called forward. An officer of the psychological warfare branch would then address the town demanding surrender of any armed forces within it. Correct treatment of prisoners and orderly occupation was promised if the surrender was made within a stipulated time. A warning was given that resistance would mean destruction of the town by shellfire. In good conditions the amplifier had a range of two miles. The words were always clear but the voice had no human quality. It came, roaring as from its metal throat — a robot threat of robot destruction surely more horrible than the sound of Joshua's trumpets to Jericho.

When the fixed defence belt had been pierced the 'inhabited place' often surrendered to the demand. The burgomaster and the commander of the loyal *Volkssturm* would come out with white flags, marching woodenly, pale-faced. But sometimes, particularly if SS men were in the town, shots would be fired. Then the tanks guns would speak. Men with dust-blackened, contorted faces would move in and out of the smoke clouds. Explosion and falling walls would thunder. A mushroom of dust based in fire would form slowly over the doomed place. Then the tanks would close in.

Some villages were almost razed this way. Better raze a village than kill a single doughboy. That was realism. The Germans had wanted war. They were getting it.

When the Remagen bridgehead was seized by surprise, held, and extended, and the tank columns which reached the Rhine near Coblenz had edged north and east again through

Andernach, most of the correspondents attached to Patton's army thought he would now make a dramatic plan and cross the big river. But he didn't. He turned south, crossing the Moselle so fast and in such strength that almost no opposition was met. This move threatened, and eventually effected, the encirclement and destruction of all that remained of the southern group of German armies.

The Moselle crossing was a brilliant, decisive move. For some reason or other — probably Patton's unpopularity with the expeditionary force command and fear in the same quarter that the neurotic and bloodthirsty general would become politically uncontrollable if he were allowed too far upstage — the operation was played down by Supreme Headquarters. It never received in the world press anything like the prominence it deserved.

When later I had a chance to analyse progress made at the time, elsewhere on the Western Front, I was convinced that Patton was still the only Allied general in the field with full realisation of what speed *blitzkrieg* could achieve. Patton took great risks to force the pace. Montgomery's British and Canadians never really got going in the north. They were cautious, uninspired. They came up against tough panzer–grenadier troops and SS. They had to fight every foot of the way.

South of them the First and Ninth US armies bungled the plan to trap all the German forces in front of Cologne and behind the Roer dams. The Germans were incomparably weaker, but they managed to get a considerable amount of equipment across the Rhine before the last bridges were demolished. In the south, the refractory, ill-equipped French played reluctant dragons round the Colmar pocket and the Seventh US army assaulted the Saar basin towns more like dynamiters than soldiers.

Out of all this an uneasy conviction arose that the coup de grâce was being given Germany not by military mastery but by an industrial sledgehammer. Patton was the only general who really got the most out of being able to deliver ten shells to the enemy's one. Disliking Patton as much as I did — his childish love of notoriety, his foul mouth, his preoccupation at his periodical press briefings with corpses — it was distasteful to admit that the man's genius as a commander in the field overshadowed that of his fellow generals. Yet the admission had to be made. The lesson seemed to be that to be a good general one must enjoy the corpses as well as Patton did; that if Britain and America ever had to fight a war without an overwhelming industrial 'edge' on the enemy, they would almost certainly lose it. Anglo-Saxon civilisation was reluctant, even in dire peril, to give its Pattons their proper stature.

I went down with the infantry into Coblenz, once a beautiful city built on a tongue of land at the confluence of the Rhine and the Moselle. It was the first really big town I had ever seen ruined to the extent that German towns were now meeting ruin. The strategic air forces had made a number of saturation bombing raids which had completely smashed about two-thirds of the built-up area. Artillery was destroying the rest.

A good deal of sniping was going on in the waterfront district. 'Watch your step,' they said at division. 'Don't drive round corners without taking a look first. The bastards on the roofs are still getting some of our boys, but you haven't got to worry about the ones down the cellars.'

On the south-eastern approaches of the city, the American troops appeared to be spread thin. There were only a few light tanks at crossroads and small groups of infantrymen exploring cellars for wine and brandy.

'Sure it's okay to go ahead. Give us a good write-up, bud! We're from Iowa...'

The marshalling yards were cratered and packed with freight waggons burned down to their framework. There were lines of empty tankers and locomotives with holes torn in their boilers.

Beyond the marshalling yards was an area of blackened and gutted loco sheds, then block after block of houses and shops and factories destroyed by bomb-blast and fire.

Toppling, plaster-stripped walls made a fantastic frieze against the smoke pall. The streets appeared very broad and bare. They were strewn with loops of electric cable, broken glass, household rubbish, rugs.

Here and there, walls had collapsed neatly cutting a section of the buildings. Sometimes bed and living rooms were dissected, the furniture still standing on the sagging floors, the crockery still on tables, the pictures still on the walls. In one second-storey room I saw the body of a man lying on a bed with his head and hands dangling.

The waterfront district was burning fiercely. German batteries on the highlands over the river occasionally dropped a shell at random in the town and our own mediums were ranged very accurately on the thin strip of shore held by the Nazi last-ditchers. The shells dropped, five or six at a time.

Smell was the insistent sense. A city under bombardment has a subtle, terrifying odour. One might almost call it a perfume. It is not unpleasant, just terrifying. It is a smell that sets the heart beating faster and the lungs labouring. It is compounded from pulverised brick, old wood burning, water on embers, smouldering flock, exploded TNT and cordite. Only later, when the city has stopped burning, does this perfume of destruction become a stink...

A sniper was firing from behind the chimneypots on the roof of a bookseller's shop. He was a marksman, and had killed or wounded seven men. He was going to be hard to deal with, so they brought up a tank. The tank fired half a dozen rounds point-blank into the building and it collapsed, spilling stone and brick across the street.

Prisoners were being rounded up from nearby cellars. Infantrymen, blear-eyed with smoke, ill-tempered with lack of sleep, moved in short rushes from building to building — prying, edging, probing the rubble for holes.

'Here, Bergman...here.' A black hole, half-stuffed with broken stone under a shopfront... Bergman ran up — a lanky man with a square, windburned face. He carried a sub-machine-gun and had a string of grenades around his neck.

'Okay. Shift 'em'… he said.

The man who had called for Bergman peered cautiously into the hole. Then he raised his head and said, 'Full of 'em.'

'Okay. Shift 'em out.'

'You down there. Come out! You got a minute to come out. You down there.' He thrust the muzzle of his carbine at random down the hole between his feet and pulled the trigger.

Bergman stood by. He snapped one of the grenades off the string round his neck, hefted it. His small brown eyes were sombre and the muscles at the corners of his jaws jumped up and down as he swallowed. Bergman wasn't planning to have any real trouble. You could see that.

A pair of white, dirty hands projecting from grey jacket cuffs came through the hole, then a helmet with a white, dirty face under it. Bergman stepped forward, snapped the helmet off and yanked the man out by his hair. 'Garn, you kraut bastard! Out of it!'

He hacked the German across the shins. The man staggered, thrust his hands as high above his head as he could get them. Thirteen Germans came out of the cellar, four wounded. Bergman kicked them all. With their hands on the backs of their necks they staggered off down the street to join dozens of other such shocked and fear-stricken bands waiting to be moved to POW cages at the rear.

I said to Bergman: 'If they don't come out, you let go with the grenades, is that right?'

'Yeh,' he said.

'Ever had occasion to let go with grenades?'

'Yeh,' he said. 'Sure thing. Three times this morning. Stubborn sons of bitches.'

A few weeks before, everyone had wondered what it would be like to occupy a big German city; and deal with kraut civilians en masse. Would they turn out to be a bunch of arrogant Nazis? Would a guy have to kick them round much? How much damage had the air raids actually done?

Well, now everybody knew the answers, but the war moved too fast for anyone to enjoy the taste of conquest. Sure it was fine to sniff out hidden wine cellars, haul bottles out of the bins and knock their necks off to sample the stuff. You could spit it out and fling the bottle against the wall if it turned out to be too dry.

Durable loot — loot you could stow in your backpack — was much harder to come by. You had to fossick for it in the canyons of rubble, or frisk corpses. There were better pickings to be had in abandoned villages.

It took the infantry several days to clear Coblenz. No news came from Remagen, so it became evident that Patton's crossing of the Moselle had been more than a feint. Some reports put Combat Command A thirty miles beyond Simmern with its reconnaissance patrols on the strategic Nahe River, west of Bad Kreuznach. The fact that it had run off its sheet maps indicated that Patton's dramatic right wheel had almost certainly been a tactical improvisation following some foul-up in Allied plans to storm across the Lower Rhine. For some reason, both Patton and Hodges were being held back from an obvious exploitation of their successes. At divisional headquarters there were rumours that Montgomery was demanding the transfer of more American divisions to the force he was assembling for the assault on the Ruhr cities after the river crossings, and that Bradley and Hodges were stubbornly opposed to any alteration in the present disposition. They were arguing that Montgomery had already screwed up the job of cleaning the Germans out of their positions on the left bank as far south as the Dortmund–Ems canal and that the main thrust should now be made in the central sector where reconnaissance had shown the German defences to be much weaker.

Patton's staff officers did not conceal their bitter dislike of Montgomery who, they declared, was determined to hog the limelight and claim to be the military genius behind the last great battle to split Germany wide open. But old Blood-and-Guts Patton still had a trick or two up his sleeve! If I wanted to see action, I should head south with the infantry.

Travelling with elements of the 5th Division I crossed the Moselle for the first time near Hartzenport. The river there was deep and swift. Steep hills covered with vineyards bore down on it. This line, resolutely defended, might have been held for months but there was little opposition in the wake of the tanks.

The slate-roofed villages in the valley were battered, but not destroyed. White flags hung from every window and civilians civilians kept discreetly out of sight. One occasionally glimpsed women peering through drawn curtains or, here and there, high on the terraced vineyards, a peasant tending vines.

The motor road along the south bank was neither blocked nor mined. Pontoon bridges fed onto it at several points. These were now guarded only by a few flak waggons and detachments of military police. They rarely knew the name of the nearest village, where the sideroads led or what lay ahead.

The German signposts were more helpful. They were always intact. I could never understand why the Germans didn't do what the British did when invasion threatened: take down all signposts and obliterate all placenames. But they never did. Nor, as far as I know, did 'intractable' Hitler Youth show initiative enough even to swivel a few signposts to mislead the enemy. It was the literal truth that the American commanders soon learned to travel as much by the face value of German roadsigns as they did by their own maps.

The Hünsruck countryside was sparsely settled. At first the villages bore few scars, though some had log road-blocks at their approaches. The tanks had bypassed them. The farms no longer had a fought-over look. The civilians were scared, but they did not have the shocked, stunned expression of villagers in the Eifel. In a few fields farmers were ploughing. Groups of women and children by the wayside hurried along without looking up at the passing enemy. I wondered where they were bound but never had time to stop and ask.

Advance elements of the 5th Division traversed the sideroads to Kastellaun, but no one in that town was sure how far the main body of armour had thrust ahead. Maybe as far as Simmern...or beyond.

No, communications weren't yet cleared. There was a bit of trouble on the flanks with small parties of Germans filtering through the forests and harrying convoys. A supply column for Combat Command B had just pulled out. If I was in a hurry I could chase it and travel with some protection.

The supply column was about ten miles on its way by the time I caught it — stalled in a traffic jam caused by a blown culvert into which a tank waggon had pitched and overturned. Frantic officers were cursing the military policemen trying to sort out the mess. It curdled my blood to imagine what a wing of fighter-bombers could have done to that tangle of shouting men and roaring machines.

A mile further on I caught up with a string of half-tracks and three Sherman tanks waddling along in the wet dusk. A precautionary rearguard for the main force?

The traffic ahead was thinning out. The road ran through a patch of pine forest, very dark and very dense, but on either side one could look for miles over farmlands and see the meagre grey spires of churches pointing upward from hidden villages. The tyres whirred soothingly.

Suddenly I noticed that the tanks ahead were veering off the road. The wheeled vehicles were pulling over. Flares blossomed above the treetops and a machine-gun fired long panicky bursts. A 88 mm shell fell in a field alongside the road, then another. Men in thin-skinned vehicles bolted for cover in the ditches where they crouched, listening for the whistle of incoming shells and flattening themselves when the projectiles dropped close by. Then the German gunners changed their fuses and began to fire black, ugly airbursts that showered the road with shrapnel.

I shared a length of ditch with a medical corpsman from a truck carrying first-aid equipment. 'The goddamn krauts know they're beaten,' he complained, 'and they want to give up. But they don't know how. They got no *machinery* for giving up. Holy tit, but a guy would be unlucky to collect his packet at this stage of the game! Airbursts, Jesus!'

After about ten minutes the tanks spotted a target and started firing. A brisk small-arms battle was developing back in the woods. Red and white flares and tracers pinpointed the area. Then a gasoline tanker took a direct hit and blew up with a gargantuan roar and blinding flashes of flame. Up the road someone started yelling for stretcher-bearers.

When the twilight faded the shelling stopped. All eagerness to catch up to the front had long since left me, but it was too late to turn back. Just before reaching the outskirts to Simmern, where I found the elusive G2 of the brigade and was assigned a billet in an undamaged house, there was another alarm. Somewhere ahead a great commotion broke out and there were yells of 'Clear it! Clear it! Combat team moving up!' Half a dozen troop-carriers roared past, their occupants festooned with grenades and ammunition belts. At the next crossroads a Sherman tank was burning and bodies of men caught in the open by automatic weapons fire were still lying on the carriageway.

Late that night there was more trouble. In the early hours the gunfire became so heavy that I climbed out of bed and went outside to investigate. The western sky was a bloody red. A village had defied the bulsh waggon and was burning.

In the morning I found out what had happened. The remnants of an SS battalion and several SP guns, retreating northward before the drive of General Patch's Seventh US army in the Palatinate, had tried to cut across our lines to Bingen, unaware that they were on a collision course with an entire armoured division. Without air reconnaissance the enemy was groping blindly for an avenue of escape. Over the next few days a score of such groups from Hitler's First Army, trapped between Patch and Patton, were surrounded and annihilated. Where, for lack of supplies or sheer wear and tear, the tanks could not keep up with the rout, swarms of fighter-bombers took over.

A Wehrmacht colonel standing by the roadside waiting for someone to accept his surrender and that of eighty stragglers with him told me: 'This is not war. You do not need tanks and guns any longer. Your aeroplanes alone could finish us.'

The third week of March brought clear spring weather — a series of sparkling, cloudless days. The squadrons of the Ninth Tactical Air Force flew twelve and thirteen hours a day on missions of execution. It *was* execution because there is no way of surrendering to a squadron of fighter-bombers diving at four hundred miles an hour. Every road and sideroad, every glade where enemy troops tried to conceal themselves, was littered with the fire-blackened wreckage. No camouflage was skilful enough, no coppice dense enough to afford protection. Where high explosive would not do the work of wrecking, then bombs charged with Napon did the job. [Napon was later to be known as napalm, a jellified mixture of naphthalene and coconut oil.] A dozen Napon bombs could turn a square mile of damp forest into an inferno.

The slaughter reached its climax east of Bad Kreuznach between 18 March and 23 March. Hundreds of German trucks, armoured vehicles and guns from the collapsed Saar Front made a dash for the Rhine. They were overtaken by swarms of American aircraft. They had much horse-drawn artillery. The Mustangs' guns piled up hillocks of dead and wounded horses and smashed limbers into which traffic speeding behind crashed.

A twenty-year-old pilot, face shrivelled into a hard squareness by his work, said: 'It was like a rat hunt. Yeh — a rat hunt. You found 'em. You beat the ground. You flushed the vermin. Then you killed it.'

Eighteen hours later I travelled a section of road where the Mustangs had found, beaten, flushed and killed. The bowels of men were looped over telephone wires by the roadside.

When a group of ten German tanks managed to gather together in a forest near Hochstetten they were attacked by five Mustangs. At the fourth pass the last fighter flew so low it crashed into the side of the only tank not yet burning.

On the night of 22–23 March, jumping the SHAEF gun by at least 48 hours and making sure that Montgomery did not upstage him, Patton sent the 5th Division over the Rhine at Oppenheim, a small town on the west bank about twenty miles due east of Bad Kreuznach and fifteen miles west of Darmstadt. Once more 'Old Blood and Guts' did the unexpected brilliantly. He changed the direction of the Third Army's drive without the slightest faltering or bungling. He thrust it like a dagger into the very vitals of central Germany, down narrow secondary roads and through bottleneck village streets. Even with opposition broken, it was a supremely daring manoeuvre and I believe it contributed substantially to shortening the war.

The 5th Division's crossing began at ten o'clock at night in bright moonlight. American air supremacy was so complete that Patton made no particular effort to conceal his concentration of men and equipment.

The ground on the rolling Rhenish plains had dried out in ten days of sunny weather. Clouds of yellow dust hung over speeding transporters loaded with pontoons, floats, assault and tank-landing craft, launches or bridging material.

During the afternoon of 22 March, all the material required for the first phase of the operation assembled undercover on the riverfront between Nierstein and Oppenheim. There was no enemy interference. Planes spotted a few enemy ammunition dumps in the fields on the far side of the river and batteries fired on them.

At nightfall squads of engineers carried several hundred light metal assault boats from their transports and ranged them behind a series of stone walls and a railway embankment about fifty yards from the water's edge. The near bank of the river shelved gently into muddy shallows. On the opposite side were reed beds and silt flats. The glare of the burning ammunition dumps was so strong that steeples in the distant villages of Geinsheim and Erfelden were visible in detail.

The river bank at Oppenheim was silent after sunset but the roar of traffic on the backroads continued. There was no artillery preparation. Spotter planes had found no worth-while targets.

At 2200 hours the infantrymen assembled near assault boats behind the embankment heard the word passed: 'Okay. On schedule. Let's go.' They lifted the boats, went down to the water, waded in, launched them, and clambered aboard.

Two hundred boats made a simultaneous crossing on a half-mile front. The stream here was between three and four hundred yards wide, with a four to six knot current. In the brilliant moonlight enfilading machine-guns could have wiped out the first wave of infantry within minutes; but there were no enfilading machine-guns.

The landings were a little further downstream than planned but the boats emptied rapidly and the men disappeared among the reeds. Twenty-three minutes after the first craft grounded in the mud a German sentry fired a shot. A grenade exploded and a flare curved up. The Third Army had its foothold on the east bank of the Rhine.

Next morning half-a-dozen Messerschmitt fighters eluded our air cover and tried to strafe the half-finished pontoon bridges. They did little damage, though the river now swarmed with Higgins boats, launches, rafts, floats, 'ducks', and even a few tank-landing craft.

Later in the day other small formations of aircraft got through the flak but failed to hit anything. Much more troublesome were some self-propelled guns dug in near Trebur. They lobbed shells at extreme range at the half-constructed heavy-duty bridge. The overs fell in the southern end of town where the houses collapsed with a crunch. It was a dismally inaccurate bombardment from which only civilians suffered.

At daybreak I went over the river in a Higgins boat, travelled for a while with a company of infantry looking for reported opposition on the Erfelden canal, and after that lay for a half an hour undercover watching the shells plopping harmlessly in the river. Then I went back to divisional headquarters. A report had just come in that patrols seven miles east of Oppenheim had not yet encountered resistance.

As soon as the heavy-duty bridge was finished the 4th Armored would pass through unchallenged.

Patton's Rhine crossing was an anticlimax, this last great military adventure of the war. A blessed anticlimax.

In the north other crossings of the Rhine were made under great barrages and the cover of thousands of aeroplanes — crossings with benefit of paratroops, chemical fog, flame-throwers, the latest and most monstrous equipment of amphibious war. The crossing in the north was an enormous fist-brandishing to claim the attention of the world and to underscore with new ruin the death sentence already spelled out by bombs. Probably the only people unimpressed by this panoply of lethal might were the men of the beaten German Army. It was simply, as the medic had said in the ditch, that they didn't have the machinery to surrender.

Chapter 5

When the Americans crushed the last German resistance in the Palatinate and the Allied armies won control of the Rhine all the way from Holland to the Swiss border, I found it physically impossible to keep up with Patton's armour and at the same time file dispatches for my newspapers. Signals, capacity stretched to the limit, could not handle low-priority traffic such as press copy. There were times when I had to make round trips of more than two hundred miles to lodge my reports with army headquarters for censorship and onward transmission. Often unit command posts had dropped thirty or forty miles behind the action, even in the Eifel and the Hünsruck where the conflict was much less diffuse than it was over the river. I would sometimes travel for an hour or more through sparsely populated areas without sighting a single American soldier.

For weeks I laboured under the delusion that this nerve-racking business of rushing back and forth to the 'front' was dangerous. Sooner or later, I thought, the German civilians would snap out of their stunned docility and start a guerrilla war. One of these fine spring mornings I was going to run into a burst of machine-gun fire or a grenade pitched out of a top-storey window...even a wire stretched from tree to tree round a sharp bend, or a nest of mines planted overnight at a crossroads. But nothing happened. The quivering tension with which I watched the road ahead, the instinctive hunch I assumed passing even through country that offered ample cover, the concentration with which I pored over ordnance maps to find routes through country officially 'cleared', were so much wasted effort.

Once, after some monumentally bad map-reading, I took a wrong road between Simmern and Trier and drove miles through a designated 'pocket of resistance'. The double-edged humour of it was the several times I hailed uniformed 'prisoners' by the roadside and demanded directions. They obliged — volubly.

After the battle for the Rhineland, the enemy no longer had the will to fight on. Hitler's armed forces waged war with a singleness of purpose and an efficiency that had enabled them to perform military miracles. His civilian population withstood terror bombing of an intensity which far surpassed that unleashed by the Luftwaffe on London, Coventry, Southhampton or any other British city. But once the British and Americans had breached the defences of the Fatherland on the ground German civilian morale collapsed totally.

Industrial cities had been so savagely mauled that the spiritless submission of their inhabitants was understandable. The attitude of the people in rural areas and small towns and villages which had escaped bombing and shelling was less comprehensible. They submitted to the authority of the invaders without question or protest — they grovelled without shame.

At first it used to make me uncomfortable to have old women scuttle off the pavement into the gutter when they saw me coming on a narrow pavement, or to see old men tip their hats and twist their lips into an ingratiating smile before answering a simple question. It used to sicken me to hear the eagerness with which the people who had made a god of Hitler and a religion of his words now denied him. If Hitler had been the Devil himself, it would still have been distasteful. Loyalty — even loyalty to a patently evil regime — can be a quality which commands respect; but there was no loyalty whatsoever to be discerned in the attitude of German civilians once their armies had been defeated and the authority of the Nazi bureaucracy destroyed. Far from creating a race of 'Supermen' the Führer's system of eliminating all opposition by keeping everybody with a pistol pointed at everybody else, had excised all real courage from the character of his people.

In one Hessian town where I occupied a billet in a requisitioned house, its owner, a woman in her fifties, had been given permission to occupy the basement. The morning after I moved in, she presented herself at the front door, wreathed in anguished smiles, and asked if she could wash any clothes for me.

I asked her who sent her. She replied that no one had sent her. I asked why she offered to do my washing — did she need money or food? She replied that she did not expect payment. I asked her why had she come? She replied that American officers had evicted her from her house, but she was not complaining. She only wished to be obliging and stand well with them. Had she been threatened or mistreated in any way? No. No. She was simply obeying orders. But she also wished to be obliging.

The rot of morale spread even into the SS. I asked one officer with a group of prisoners of war on the road near Fulpa about the recruiting system for the elite SS. With tears in his eyes, he whined: 'Why do you think we are any different from Wehrmacht? It was a voluntary arm of the services at the beginning of the war, but not later. We were conscripted. We only obeyed our orders like any soldier. Why should our heads have to fall for that?'

Here was a man who, a week previously, would no doubt have died for his country — *but only at the direct order of a superior officer*. When the chain of command broke, there were no inward resources, no pride, no faith to sustain his courage. He was an animal trained to act on reflex to given stimuli. Switch the stimuli and he was bewildered and lost — an intellectually impotent and confused rat in a strange laboratory maze.

The only even mildly humorous example of the Germans' unquestioning obedience to authority I came across was at

Mainz. Sniping from an upper window was holding up clearance of a suburban block. Infantrymen were waiting round for the inevitable tank to come and do the job, when a massive woman, waving a white flag on a broomstick, emerged from the house opposite that from which the sniping was coming. She crossed the road and disappeared inside. In five minutes she emerged, leading the snipers by their ears. They were her sons, aged twelve and fourteen, who were obeying the order of their Hitler Youth group leader to die like valiant young werewolves — until mother asserted the more direct authority.

After the encirclement of Model's divisions in the Ruhr, the only doubt about the outcome of the war was when it would end. I am convinced that if the German people had shown the spirit to wage a partisan campaign behind the Allied spearheads which split the country, or if the German general staff had been able or willing to regroup and concentrate substantial forces in the Bavarian mountains, Hitler would have made good his last maniacal promise to bring all Europe down in chaos should his arms fail.

Anyone who chased Patton's tanks and motorised infantry to Chemnitz or, for that matter, followed the thrusts westward from the Middle Rhine towards Berlin, could not have failed to realise how desperately thin on the ground the forces of occupation were spread. They hadn't the manpower to control a hostile civilian population.

The towns and villages of central Germany were not very different from the towns and villages of the Rhineland. But after Kassel fell, resistance diminished to an occasional defiant twitch. Now and again a village would defy the bulsh waggon and the guns would bark, but that happened less and less frequently. White flags still hung out of windows days after the last Allied tanks had passed through. There was no sabotage or sniping at supply columns — or even at lone travellers tagging along behind in jeeps and command cars.

Only when truckload after truckload of Wehrmacht prisoners started to come down the line did I discover that more than a sense of final defeat caused this almost eerie passivity. East of the Elbe, division after division of Hitler's army threw down their weapons and fled across the river to escape the remorselessly advancing Russians. Any fate was preferable to the fate that awaited the German soldier who surrendered to the hordes of Tartary!

Berlin, 1945
Photograph: Osmar White

Part III

INSIDE
HITLER'S
REICH

Chapter 6

A traveller with the Allied armies that dissected the body of Germany in 1945 often came across physical evidence that shed new light on Nazi psychology. Fear and guilt were buried under the strident arrogance of the *Herrenvolk*.

As though they had a presentiment of ultimate defeat before they embarked on their attempt to conquer Europe, Hitler's gangsters were busily burrowing vast and elaborate underground warrens in which to hide if things went wrong.

These were not in the ordinary sense of the term fortifications of the sort that had been built in the Maginot and Siegfried Lines. They were isolated boltholes designed to afford selective shelter for the elite of the regime and its helots.

The first of these I saw was the oldest — the Führer's general headquarters at Ziegenhain, west of Bad Hersfeld. When Patton's tanks ripped north from Frankfurt towards Kassel in early April they overran the place almost without noticing it. It was a fair-sized town, drilled and blasted under a mountainous ridge flanking the Berlin–Frankfurt highway. Hitler had directed the invasion of the Low Countries and France from its map-room in 1940. And there, four years later, von Rundstedt watched the progress of the Ardennes offensive.

Ziegenhain's approaches were unobtrusive sideroads leading off the autobahn. The countryside was charming, chequered with green fields in the village between densely wooded ridges.

Some of the old-world villages were what they seemed to be. Some weren't. They were clusters of pillboxes and gun emplacements with reinforced concrete walls and deep, steel-beamed cellars, but their facsimile of 500-year-old architecture was perfect. One entire farm was not a farm at all, but a small elaborately equipped airport, its buildings disguised as haystacks and barns.

Allied intelligence knew that the German headquarters were hereabouts and heavy bombers blasted the area. The bombs fell on the just and unjust alike, so village after village, genuine and fake, was pulverised.

The castle of Ziegenhain under which the central fort had been excavated was almost totally demolished. All that was left of the lavishly restored tenth-century building was one jagged wall and the base of its round tower. Blockbusters had smashed fifteen-foot-thick ramparts to powder.

The road, an uncambered twenty-foot driveway, app-roached the castle through the village of Ziegenhain itself, skirted the hill whereon the castle's ruin stood and then plunged off into forest. Camouflage nets stretched among the trees and young firs had been trained to grow through and over them. In small, log-lined pits sentries had kept guard, only their heads showing above ground.

According to the villagers the Führer used to walk on this road in the evening with his bodyguard posted at twenty-yard intervals, backs turned. Among the trees was the wreckage of a lighting plant which must have given the place a pantomime-fairyland appearance at night. Each globe was tinted and shaded to give no upward glare. Only when the radar station gave warning of approaching aircraft were these lights turned off.

The road passed a long, rustic lodge — a barracks for junior SS officers — and led to a scattering of buildings which at first glance looked like the remains of solidly built country cottages, but which were really entrances to the 'bunkers' of the fort. Here party and army dignitaries had lived, guests of Hitler, who occupied 'Haus No. 1'.

When the place was evacuated squads of soldiers had been ordered to demolish everything that could be demolished. They had gone through the bunkers with drums of gasoline, dynamite and flamethrowers, but enough was left in the charred rubbish to see that the houses had once been luxuriously furnished.

The cellar stairs in each were labelled with the sign that one saw all over Germany: '*ZUM LUFTSCHUTZRAUM*'. The '*Luftschutzraum*' in this case was the fortress itself.

A single floor down, and all reality was left behind. A maze of concrete passageways led down into the mountain's roots. The doors were of heavy metal with peepholes of bulletproof glass in them. There were the remains of electric eye and supersonic detection devices, and of microphones set into the ceilings of guest rooms, of innumerable escape trapdoors and recesses for sentries, and secret exits. Fear and suspicion, carried to the limits of human imagination, were the only emotions which could have motivated the design of this place. It was a place where men had prepared to hide themselves from the wrath of their fellow men in a robot world carved out of living rock. It had been ventilated, warmed, lighted and drained with insane ingenuity. Its whole atmosphere was the atmosphere of an aseptic, plush-padded torture chamber — a torture chamber in which the torturer was the mind, the conscience of those who created and occupied it. Everything could be shut out — everything except fear.

Beneath the bunker houses three levels of chambers linked seven further levels below Ziegenhain Castle. Intelligence officers estimated that the complex could have provided accommodation for at least 3000 people.

I spent a couple of afternoons exploring the empty, echoing passageways and rooms. Bats were already flying through them. It was an eerie, edgy business. Every now and then one trod, cat-footed, on trapdoors which gave slightly, or came suddenly on apartments labelled with infamous names: Himmler, Goebbels, Goering, Kesselring. There were vaults which contained smashed radio transmitters, telephone switchboards, diesel generating plants, machinery for sewage disposal and water reticulation. There were kitchens, bathrooms, map-rooms and a great library knee-deep in torn and defaced books and manuscripts. Acrid ammoniac fumes from the wrecked airconditioning plant were beginning to creep into the lower tunnels.

The villagers living in the cellars under the rubble of their homes had come sneaking in as soon as the demolition parties left, to loot what remained of furniture, fittings and tools. They told fanciful stories about the fortress and its occupants, but obviously knew little about what actually went on there. The work had been completed in 1939. Concentration-camp labour had been used. Many workers had died.

One villager claimed to have been a servant at the castle until 1943. When the war was going well he said, the SS gave wild parties. All the big names in Germany came to visit. He showed me an enormous dump of empty champagne, brandy and liqueur bottles in the forest. He told a long, maundering story about Hitler's habits and appearance, and described — probably more accurately — the big bombing raid of 27 March, when a direct hit wrecked Kesselring's bunker house. Several staff officers were killed and the general himself slightly wounded by flying glass when a chandelier crashed on the table at which he was sitting.

Yet far more memorable than the villagers' facts, fictions and half-fictions was the valediction of an old man sitting on the doorstep of his broken cottage: 'They have gone away and left us alone,' he muttered. 'They have brought Germany to ruin. But thanks to God they have gone away, and they will leave us alone for all time.'

The underground hide-out motif was repeated through all Germany. Later I saw armament and aircraft factories in old salt mines where thousands of slave-workers had fed the Nazi war machine with their labour and their lives. They were uncanny impressive caverns but they were logical improvisations to protect war industry from the increasing weight of air attack. Britain might have found the same use for old mine workings if pressed hard enough.

What on the other hand was 'super-normal' was the way in which the Nazis had — long before there was any apparent reason for believing that Germany would be forced to a last-ditch defence — anticipated the requirements for physical survival under atomic bomb attacks.

Ziegenhain, the headquarters of the *Oberkommando der Wehrmacht* (OKW) near Gotha, and the labyrinths under Berchtesgaden and Reichschancellery in Berlin were vast works planned in detail ten to twelve years before conventional explosives dropped from the sky began to disrupt the nation's industrial and administrative machinery. At first one was inclined to attribute their existence to an insane fixation on the elaborate, dramatic and fantastic in the minds of those who had them built. They were comic-strip creations, designed by adolescents but adolescents with the power to command technical genius and limitless labour and wealth to give substance to their crazy dreams.

Later one wondered if these 'adolescents' had not possessed some gift of prophetic vision of a world inhabited by men who had wrung every secret from nature, if not the secret of how to control their own lust for power over other men.

These first burrowings of a diseased civilisation driving itself underground were more interesting than important in the kind of war then being fought. The treasure, genius, sweat and blood they cost the German people contributed, in the long run, little or nothing to the defence of the country. Only the Berlin Chancellery was defended, and that did not give the Russians very much trouble because the general organisation of the defenders had collapsed long before the Chancellery came under shellfire. If instead of a few trainloads of Party records, the equipment at Peenemunde laboratories had been housed beneath the Adlerhorst at Berchtesgaden, the end of the war might have been different. If from the start Hitler had given priority to atom bomb research and if he had centred it in the Bavarian Redoubt and defended the area as it could have been defended, he might have blasted Europe into submission from a Germany reduced by invasion to an area of a few hundred square miles.

There are many 'ifs' about the Second World War, but these, to my mind, are the 'ifs' which can most profitably be studied by the strategists of the future.

Without knowing anything about the race between Anglo-Americans and Nazi scientists to perfect the atom bomb, many military observers who visited the Redoubt were puzzled why Hitler didn't opt for defence-to-the-death there. Why, if he did really commit suicide in the sordid rubble of Berlin, did he choose that death instead of the spectacular end he could have made among the mountains? The reduction of an Alpine defence pocket with Berchtesgaden as its nerve centre would have cost the Allied armies great effort, months of time, and probably thousands of lives.

From a military point of view the series of interlocked valleys about Berchtesgaden is one of the most inaccessible regions in Germany. All the approaches are through narrow, winding passes among the mountains 6000 or 7000 feet high. Alpine streams thunder in the gorges. There are patches of dense forest and hillsides riddled with old mine workings for cover and concealment. It is country of scenic grandeur — and a military tactician's nightmare. Guns well placed in the hills could have made the roads impassable to armour for as long as they had shells to fire. Large demolitions, instead of a few inexpertly blown bridges, would have destroyed rather than cut many approaches. They would have sponged out the ledges on which roads were built across the faces of sheer precipices.

I went into Berchtesgaden first from the Munich side. My companion was a New Zealand major seasoned in mountain fighting by that long, strategically useless grind up the Apennines from Cassino. After a couple of days travelling, during which he said very little and saw a great deal, he pronounced verdict on the Redoubt. He said: 'I'm damned glad Adolf didn't decide to shack up here with a survival kit. If he had, it would have taken another six months to crack him. It would have been a job for mountain troops alone. All the armour and air in the world would have made no difference.'

Berchtesgaden town itself showed few scars, only bomb craters in the railroad yards and a house or two knocked down by admonitory shellfire. True, it looked bedraggled, but it had an air of tranquillity. The milky-green mountain stream rushed boisterously by the side of the highway. The grass on the vacant lots and in the gutters was spangled with daisies.

We slept that night in the Summer Chancellery where the 101st Airborne Division had set up headquarters. The Chancellery was about two miles out of town on the Salzburg road, a low, single-storey building in the modern style. It contained a series of offices, work, reception and living rooms which were decorated and furnished with more restraint and in better taste than the majority of Nazi public buildings. There were (wonder of wonders in Germany) cheerfully coloured paintings and prints on the walls. Everything was functional, comfortable and decently subdued. Nazi love of *Wunder* was apparent only when one went through the innocent-looking doors at the end of side corridors and descended into white-walled tunnels zigzagging steadily downward.

The chambers they served were designed on a far less lavish scale than those beneath Ziegenhain, but their purpose was the same: to provide completely bombproof housing for a control organisation. There were combined offices and sleeping quarters, dining and rest rooms, storage depots, repair shops and all the now familiar machinery for servicing a subterranean town. The service plant had not been destroyed and it was possible to get some idea of what life in such a place would be like. The airconditioner diesels whirred softly. Hundreds of powerful but diffused lights gleamed in the ceilings.

Some of the staff had apparently taken up permanent or semipermanent residence in anticipation of heavy bombing after the attack on Hitler's Obersalzburg compound a few miles away. Most of the furniture had been wantonly smashed by the French troops who had beaten the Americans to Berchtesgaden by a few hours, but one could deduce from the wreckage that comfort had been achieved.

Life here, I thought, was probably not as depressing as it might be. There was little sense of being shut in, no chill and damp. There were no recesses for machine-gunners, no peepholes and no electric eyes. The refuge was intended primarily for underlings, who presumably needed no such surveillance.

The Nazis no doubt intended eventually to link up this series of shelters with the far more elaborate works beneath Obersalzburg and the Adlerhorst, a concrete blockhouse on the summit of 6000-foot Mount Kehler.

I went up the mountainside to look at the remains of the most publicised of Hitler's 'houses'. In March the RAF had staged a publicity (or maybe an experimental?) raid, dropping 4000-pound bombs. The world had long been familiar with the likeness of the squat, ugly retreat where the Führer spent his vacations; the outsized study with the outsized fireplace and the outsized window framing the view across the valley; the inevitable SS barracks, the storehouses, the guest lodges, the dance and dining halls set about the barracks square; the once beautiful little village strangled by a cancer of concrete and steel ostentation.

Now only fire-blackened walls, slabs of stone, piles of cinders, rubbish, rags, blowing papers were left. The mountain-side was torn by craters in the yellowish earth. Even sections of pine forest were stripped by blast to stark dead sticks.

Beneath this chilling evidence of what orthodox bombing could do on the surface, the shelters were intact.

The Adlerhorst itself — the eyrie on the mountain — had not been bombed. Parts of the road leading up to it were literally no more than deep notches carved in vertical cliff faces. Two long tunnels and three lesser ones reduced the steepest pinches in an overall gradient of 4000 feet in five miles.

Four hundred feet below the tip of the peak a roundabout marked the end of the carriageway. Spring had melted the last snowdrifts into curved shapes on the flanks of the bronze doors giving access to elevators at the foot of the last precipice.

The approaches were guarded by gum-chewing, bored paratroopers.

'No,' one of them said. 'You gotta walk up, outside. No, you can't take a look. There's twenty levels of f----g air-raid shelter in there, and every level's lousy with booby traps. The engineers are taking it steady, and they won't be cleared for weeks.'

I walked up, slowly.

Over there, in Austria, the River Inn coiled through alpine meadows, north and west was the Steinig Meer — the ocean of stone — its grey-mauve peaks flecked with snow. A place of thin, many-tongued winds and dizzy gulfs. South and below lay Berchtesgaden's faery valley where the fields were afire with daisies, gentians, wild primula and alpine roses.

This was where the man who enslaved a nation, poisoned its soul, and desolated a continent, came to find inspiration!

Here in a hexagonal chamber with granite walls five feet thick and marble flagstones at its doors, he plotted with his disciples.

The room was panelled in golden oak. Its ceiling was thirty feet high. In its chimney-place an ox could turn on the spit. Its circular centre table was twenty-five feet in diameter and covered by a cloth of seamless chenille. Next to it was a banqueting room with seats for sixty guests, lighted by two crystal chandeliers and furnished with orange and gold Meissen china, plate and solid silver. The adjoining kitchen twinkled with chrome and tiles and copper cooking pans, ranges, refrigerators and marble workbenches.

All this on a mountain top. It was strange, but the opulence did not impress. It was strange, but one was not stimulated even to think much about the man who planned it.

The windows were the clue to the paradox — the windows through which the mountains looked in with utter indifference. The wonder came from the texture of the distant snowpeaks rather than from the smooth intricacy of the inlaid floor; from the hypnotic emerald of Köningssee set in its piney gorges, rather than from the diamantine glitter of the chandeliers.

Hitler sought here to convince himself and the world that he was a great man because he could order slaves to build a palace on the top of a mountain. How the god of the mountain must have grinned when five years of prodigious effort ended in 1938 and the Adlerhorst was finished!

The Führer's fabulous pimple on the Bavarian peak was less impressive than many a public lavatory! A goatherd's chalet, perched on the lip of its waterfall, more dominated its surroundings and better expressed the dignity of its tenant.

I came down from the Adlerhorst profoundly flat in spirit. The evil Colossus who had bestridden Europe was a little man — the kind of man who failing all else carves his name on glacial boulders to make sure he will be remembered.

Chapter 7

Not surprisingly, the Nazi hierarchs who sought to assure their personal survival by creating an underworld to which they could retreat if ever threatened by the Allies, chose to conceal their booty in subterranean hiding places. In the last weeks of the war they scuttled madly from place to place hiding what they had stolen in caves, mines, wells and cemetery vaults.

American forces in central and southern Germany unearthed 53 deposits of Nazi loot in April and early May.

The treasure was delivered into the custody of the United States Group Council at Frankfurt. It filled every available foot of storage space in the great Reichsbank building. Probably never before had such a collection of what men call wealth been under one roof. The chief item was bullion to the value of several thousand million dollars including the entire Reichsbank reserve and the greater part of the Hungarian Treasury's silver stocks. There were hogsheads full of precious stones. There were barrels of silver and gold watches, jewellery of every kind, and long 'sausages' of threaded wedding rings stripped from the hands of women in concentration camps. Grislier still were wooden cases packed with the gold and silver fillings taken from the teeth of murdered Jews and Poles — the contribution of Himmler's men to 'organisational funds'. A whole room at the Frankfurt bank was piled, ceiling high, with paper currency in canvas bags, and another room with negotiable securities from almost every country in the world.

Elsewhere were art treasures stolen or 'bought' at pistol point all over Europe. The great gangsters were jealous of their reputation for culture.

Six months later, officials of the United States Treasury and the Bank of England were still working to determine ownership of many items in the vast hoard. Apportionment of any unidentified balance was to be the subject of agreement by the Powers concerned in the final peace settlement.

The discovery of the first half-dozen caches caused excitement and speculation among the invading troops, but finding, guarding, and eventually transporting gold bars and crates of old masters soon became one of the more tiresome and exacting tasks of the occupation army.

I was in a nearby town when the Reichsbank's hoard at Merkers was discovered — one of the more 'respectable' concealments, because it had been undertaken for a state institution rather than a private individual.

During the evening of 7 April the young public relations officer of the 90th Infantry Division, pale with excitement, announced after briefing that the division had captured the Third Reich's entire gold reserve sealed up in a rock-salt chamber 2000-feet deep in the Kaiseroda mine near Merkers. Three officials of the State Bank headed by Director Fritz Vieck were now prisoners in the village. They said that at least a hundred tons of gold bricks and millions of dollars worth of German and foreign paper currency was hidden in the mine. The chamber where the gold was supposed to be stashed had not yet been broken into. It was bricked up and entry was a demolition job, but there was no reason to doubt the treasure was there. One of the directors of the Berlin Museum, P.O. Rave, had also been captured. He had said millions of dollars worth of art treasures and rare manuscripts was also in the mine and he had led senior divisional officers to the galleries where the crates were stacked.

The next morning every pressman in camp lit out in a cutthroat race, to see the blowing of the treasure chamber door. Merkers was a more than usually ugly mining village dominated by the poppet heads and brick stacks of the great saltworkings beneath it. Some of the mines were among the oldest in Germany and went down to depths of more than 3000 feet.

Kaiseroda was not much different from the rest — a collection of iron sheds to house machinery, brick and concrete office buildings, and barracks, all surrounded by barbed wire.

Division had by now become oppressively conscious of its responsibility. Machine-gun emplacements were liberally scattered over the landscape. Correspondents were held up at the main gates while the brigadier was run to earth. He was the only man, the guard said, who could authorise inspection.

Several hundred British and South African war prisoners who had been employed in the mine were standing about watching proceedings with sardonic interest. I talked to a group for a while and then said casually: 'I don't suppose any of you fellows knew about the treasure down here. The jerries must have kept it pretty quiet.'

They were surprised.

'Gawd,' said one hefty Cockney, 'the whole bleedin' countryside knew about it. DPs and all! It was a DP that tipped off these bleedin' Yanks!'

'But,' I asked incredulously, 'if you knew all the gold in Germany was down that mine, didn't you go to the officer commanding the troops who first came here and tell him what you knew?'

The stolid Briton shrugged. 'Wasn't none of my business. Couple of sergeants *did* report it to the MPs three or four days ago, but the MPs never did a bleedin' thing. Thought the sergeants was batty, I suppose...'

This story was quite true. When the 90th Division hit Merkers it was travelling too fast to be worried about a couple of 'Limey lunatics' with a story about all the gold in Germany. What had happened was this:

On the night of 5 April a military policeman on patrol had seen two French women on the road. It was after curfew and he asked for their permits to be out. They had none. They said they were looking for a midwife. A friend of theirs was about to have a baby. The policeman thought this was a somewhat phoney story and said he would walk back with them to the DP centre to check. On the way the women asked what the Americans were going to do with all that treasure in the salt mine. The policeman was disbelieving again, but the women were so insistent about both the baby and the treasure that he decided the time had come for a good, conscientious MP to pass the buck. In time the matter came to the ears of the unit CO, who had made further inquiries. Everybody in town was amazed at such ignorance. Of course there was treasure in the salt mine — the gentlemen in charge of it were staying at the local hotel! And so they were — three prim men in black, clerkly coats, wearing eyeglasses and short haircuts. They were frank. They disclosed all with an air of undisguised relief.

After checking this piquant tale, a few correspondents managed to infiltrate the Kaiseroda wire under cover of the divisional general and half-a-dozen staff officers who had come to see the incredible for themselves.

We all got into a rickety elevator operated by a pair of the most villainous-looking miners I have ever set eyes on. The machinery clanked and the cage plunged giddily down through the darkness. Some tactful soul said in a reflective tone: 'What a chance for a werewolf! A couple of stars, a brace of chickens, a whole goddamn treeful of leaves, and the cream of the world's press — all for the price of a file and ten minutes' quiet work!'

I thought gloomily about a 'prophecy piece' I had written the day before in which I had opined that the Germans would never carry the fight underground.

Another German miner let us out of the cage at the 2100 feet level. We entered a roomy, rather cheerful-looking gallery in the salt seam. It was lit by bright electric lights. A cut-out sign said 'HEIL HITLER!'; and another, 'THY STRENGTH IS NOTHING: THE PEOPLE'S STRENGTH IS ALL!'

Two or three hundred yards down a side gallery were two sour-looking American sentries with carbines, a jammed vault door, and a neat hole blown in the brick sealing of the mouth of a recess.

The treasure chamber was dimly lighted. It receded into shadow. Its floor was almost entirely covered with little, red-sealed canvas bags. We did not touch them at first but made a solemn count — 27 rows, 157 bags in each row, plus 283 miscellaneous bags.

'Open one of them,' said the general.

A staff officer jerked the seals off a bag, fumbled, pulled out a gold brick. The general hefted it. We all hefted it — and handed it back to the general.

Yes...fifty pounds, near enough. The hundred-ton estimate was not so far wrong. The general was sweating profusely.

'Hold it, General!'

Flashlights exploded.

'Hold it, General...'

'Here, General...these ones have got gold francs in them... See?'

The general was now streaming with sweat.

'That's enough,' he snapped. 'Now for God's sake let's get out of here!' His stern disappeared rapidly through the hole.

'Ah!' said the correspondent of Agence France Presse, blowing a kiss at the bag parade. 'Oh, to be invisible! Just for one little, little moment to be invisible!'

Outside, shifting from one foot to the other, the State Bank director Fritz Vieck was waiting. His expression was a mixture of anxiety and resignation. He answered questions crisply. He said that the treasure had been transferred from Berlin in the five weeks beginning 11 February. It had been brought here in military trucks by the Wehrmacht. It was then believed that Berlin would have to be evacuated and one would not wish it to fall into Russian hands.

'When we crossed the Rhine, didn't you make an effort to get the stuff out of here?' someone asked.

'Yes,' Vieck said, 'an order was received to remove as much of the paper money as possible. It was needed for immediate war purposes. The Reichsbank printing presses had been destroyed by bombing. But the Americans had moved too fast and the roads were too dangerous.' He refused to give an estimate of the value of this treasure in marks.

Someone else asked: 'What effect do you think the capture of this mine will have on the prosecution of the war?'

Vieck's eyes were sombre. 'None,' he said. 'None — any more.' Then with a suggestion of arrogance, 'Of course, afterwards it will do much to stabilise the value of the mark.'

He led us a few steps to the gallery where the paper money was stacked in neat white sacks, each stamped with the mark value of the currency contained therein — interminable rows of meaningless noughts. The procession of inspection solemnly kicked or punched the bags as it passed.

At the end of the stack was a small, gentle-faced man in a rumpled grey suit, sitting disconsolately on a couple of million dollars. He was watched unwinkingly by his escort, an unshaven PFC from Maryland. He was the museum director. His name was Rave. With weary courtesy he showed us crate after crate of Greek, Chinese and Egyptian ceramics, packing cases full of canvases by Menzel, Dürer, Manet, Constable, Raphael, Titian, Van Dyct, da Vinci — coffers in which were packed the manuscripts and relics of Goethe, loose albums with engravings, etchings and drawings by the masters of all nations. They were stacked on the naked floor with salt softly falling on them.

Speaking rapid, bad French, Rave said he believed about one-quarter of the art treasures collected by the German state were now stored here. The evacuation of the Berlin Museum had been planned four or five months ago, but in the end the job had been done so hurriedly that he had come away with incomplete lists.

I was sorry for Rave. I think he was just an expert, completely wrapped up in his speciality, eighteenth-century painting. He faced the barrage of newspaper questions with admirable courage.

One alert Midwesterner thought he was on a winning vein when he asked was Menzel a Jew.

'*Mein Gott, mon dieu*!' Rave exclaimed.

An even more alert New Yorker asked: 'Have you any statues by Epstein here?'

Rave replied, a glint in his eyes: 'Epstein? Ah, yes, I have heard of him. Very abstract, is he not?'

We left the man sitting on his sacks of banknotes, moistening his lips. I could not forbear fraternisation. I said: 'Well, I hope we meet again in happier circumstances, Herr Rave.'

He smiled faintly and bowed, very stiffly.

After that we all went back to the cage and shot up at a speed which set the ears cracking, and then out into the bright spring morning. A Thunderbolt passed across the clear sky leaving a comet's tail of vapour. A gun boomed in the distance. The submachine-gunners were sitting drowsily in the sunshine.

A philosopher next to me shook the salt dust from his shirt and said, 'Well that's that. So what? Funny, but you can't eat it, you can't wear it, you can't fire it out of guns. You can't even burn most of it. What the hell has all the excitement been about?'

In the next few weeks the bottom fell out of the market in buried treasure stories. Hoard after hoard was discovered. The hunt moved south, into the flowering meadows and the gloomy gorges of the Tyrolean and Bavarian highlands. Almost daily, detachments of troops set out to follow up some tip. Ten years of living under Hitler had convinced the Germans that informing pays. They fairly scampered to betray the trust of their old masters, moved not nearly so much by hatred of them as by the hope of currying favour with the new. There was no real need to go out and look for Nazi loot. One only had to sit still and wait. In time some shifty-eyed character would come into the Military Government office, twisting his cap between his hands. He would be quivering with information about suspicious characters and mysterious goings-on at old mines in the mountains.

The troops soon lost all capacity for amazement. Treasure? Well? The war was over around here and the valleys were dreaming in the sun. Cattle were grazing knee-deep in flowers. Nazi loot? Look for it? Better sit looking at the mountains and rivers and lakes — and pretty Bavarian girls in peasant costume. Looking was work and trouble...

Robert Ley, boss of Nazi labour, assigned a detachment of specially trusted SS men to guard his private cache. They fell out among themselves in their salt mine when bored doughboys arrived, exploded a few grenades by way of warning, and accepted the surrender of all three factions of snarling watchdogs. The first faction had wanted to make the super-gesture and blow up the whole mine; the second wanted only to blow up the art and plant the coin; the third wanted to go to the Americans and try to swap information for preferential treatment as prisoners.

One morning I went to see Hermann Goering's collection. The 101st Airborne Division had rescued it from the wet mine where it was hidden and stored it in a white-walled workman's resthouse a few miles from Berchtesgaden. Divisional headquarters said a rough valuation of the paintings, statuary and jewellery in that house was one hundred million dollars. The building was guarded by a company of dreamy-eyed paratroopers.

Inside, Goering's 'purchasing' adviser, Walter Andreas Hofer, was brooding happily over the pictures that had been removed from the mine just in time to save them from irreparable damage by damp. Hofer was a middling sized man on the wrong side of fifty, with puckered up blue eyes, a blotchy skin, and a stoop. He had once been a famous art dealer in Berlin, but since 1933 he had been Goering's trained magpie. His faded, colourless wife was an expert restorer, and while I was talking to her, she went imperturbably on with the work of removing a mildew mark from the surface of Vermeer's *Christ and the Adulteress*.

Hofer was delighted to show off the choice titbits he had bought his master. A large bedroom was almost filled with unframed canvases and panels. Hofer shuffled amongst them with gentle haste, peering, tilting, commenting in thick English, his spatulate fingertips exploring the paint anxiously for blemishes.

This room alone, he said, contained seven Rubens pieces, including the most famous of that painter's crucifixions. He slid it out and turned it to the light. 'Ah!' he said delightedly, 'is it not superb!'

I looked, and felt a wave of nausea. Rubens had seen torture. Rubens must have seen torture. No one who had not seen torture could have painted that crucifixion — the body of a man with knotted sinews and the little blood vessels in his nose burst with the violence of the cry, 'Why hast thou forsaken me?'

Hofer tittered. 'And here...very amusing. Very — what do you say? — hot.' He propped Boucher's erotic masterpieces painted for the bedchamber of Madame Pompadour to titillate the flagging passions of Louis — massive pink women being borne naked to bed, squealing.

Hofer moved the canvases for half an hour, talking about art and Goering and the wicked tricks of collectors. He was quite frank about his relationship with the Luftwaffe chief. He liked him. He was jolly, generous... Now here were altar pieces by Wilhelm von Köln and some Andrea del Sarto panels. Beautiful, beautiful! Of course everything was bought. No appropriation. Goering knew nothing about art when he started. He just wanted to do the right thing and have a collection like other important men. This was a folio of Dürer drawings. Here were five Rembrandts — quite priceless. Yes, everything was bought and paid for. There would be no trouble at all about proving the legality of purchases. Some collectors had been reluctant to part with their pieces, but Goering was always content to wait within reason, and increase his offer, if necessary. Van Dyct's *Portrait of a Family*. Exquisite, no? Ah, what magic in that brush... These Holbeins... Goering had really got quite good at it in the end. He developed an almost unerring sense for what was important in art. In later years he had developed even taste! Yes, possibly taste for figure drawing and nudes. Here? A Bellini. Yes, a Bellini. There had been quite an art rivalry between Goering and Hitler. Sometimes they bid against each other. Friendly, of course. No one could buy pictures on this scale for twelve years without learning something about the business...

In the end a guard came into the room and said: 'The major says you'd better let this kraut get back to work. He's got plenty to do relisting this stuff.'

Hofer straightened, shrugged, smiled depreciatingly. 'Ah, war!' he said. 'Goodbye, goodbye. It has been pleasant to talk to an Englishman again. I am very fond of the English.'

The next room was full of marble nudes, life-size terracottas of the Virgin Mary, satyrs, saints, warriors and legendary beasts. In the next were platoons of gold, silver and porcelain figurines. Near the main entrance was a sitting room in which Goering's personal plate and trophies were stacked, gold and chased silver dishes, antique cabinets inset with precious stones. Loving cups, chalices, medals, decorations and insignia, ceremonial swords and maces, books and vellum-bound addresses with the bindings studded with gems.

Even Goering, the jolly, reasonable, bluff Goering — the one lovable monster — had walled up his swag in a hole where water could deface priceless paint, tarnish metal, rot the wood of ancient panels. Instinct is powerful... Run and hide it, run and hide it. Bury it. Run and hide everything but the shapes in the mind.

Hitler, they say, died with his mistress after a death feast in a labyrinth-room. Himmler gritted the poison vial and swallowed and felt the life ebb out of him in convulsions. Others strangled themselves, or died by the gun. Some were destined to sit in cells, waiting, and go to weary endless questionings to satisfy the form of Justice. Some were silent. Some were mad. *'Don't you remember me, Hess? I am Hermann Goering. I was chief of the Luftwaffe...'*

Flight and capture. Capture and death, and beyond death, if Jehovah does repay, flight again down the corridors of eternity lit by electric globes and studded with electric eyes, then warm, washed air heavy with the rhythm of machinery, their shadows shaped in the likeness of Ruben's crucified Man.

Chapter 8

Roads flying back under the jeep wheels... Roads that led, narrow as canyons, through rolling forests of pines and oaks and beeches, putting on new green coats. Roads through battered towns and silent villages, winding among fields and lunging down over streams. Broad, smooth autobahn, tarred highways, clay trails... Roads crowded with traffic and roads so lonely they even seemed to promise escape from the evil that men did.

Whenever in the future I recall the spring of 1945, I know I shall first remember the roads on which one sometimes had leisure to think as well as to see.

After the fighting moved north and east from Frankfurt, I used to tell myself: 'One of these days if you keep on following your nose you'll end up in a concentration camp.'

I used to wonder what a concentration camp would be like. I already knew, of course. Anybody who could read knew what a concentration camp was like — had known for years. It was a place where the SS exterminated Jews in gas chambers, where they beat prisoners with rubber hoses or worked them until they dropped dead.

Of course I knew. There was already literature on such places, but I still wondered.

Sometimes in timbered country the way ran past grim, green-painted hutments surrounded by barbed wire. Perhaps these might have once been concentration camps? They had an atmosphere of cruelty and menace.

Intelligence reports received at this time said that the Nazis were frantically trying to evacuate all camps threatened by the invading armies. There were tales of death marches, of columns of starving and exhausted prisoners lashed along by SS guards. They were being taken to the Bavarian Redoubt as hostages. Hitler was going to say: 'Make a deal with me, or I will kill all these people.' As one tale went, the pilot of a low-flying fighter saw a procession of Jewish women being driven by SS women with whips. But, predictably, no one could find the pilot or knew his squadron...

I confess to doubts about concentration camps — not that they existed or that they were centres of mass murder and torture; but I suspected that propagandists had magnified and distorted the brutality of a sadistic political prison system. The horror stories of 1914 came to mind — the factory in which corpses were boiled down for soap, Belgian babies impaled on German bayonets, wounded soldiers crucified. In time of war civilians are willing to believe any rumour about the bestiality of the enemy.

When the armour turned east along the Leipzig autobahn from Hersfeld someone said: 'Well, this is the concentration camp country.' True.

Weimar fell. A woman who claimed to have an American mother interpreted for the burgomaster when he was being interrogated after the surrender. Later she answered questions for the press. In a shrill, superior voice she harped on about the little city's great cultural tradition, and its claim to special consideration as the home of Goethe, Schiller and Liszt. 'Of course,' she complained, 'your bombers always managed to hit some cultural edifice!'

My billet was a rich house near the park where Liszt's garden cottage stands. It was full of solid, comfortable furniture. It had well-stocked bookshelves and a garden that had been lovingly tended. It seemed to have belonged to an educated and reflective man — a stodgy man perhaps, but one who used life's good things with decent moderation. Over the bed in my room was a coloured print of Goethe in Napoleonic stance, radiating lofty intelligence and sensibility. It also contained a massive dry point of two lovers in a forest glade. The title, in flowing script, was: *AM BUCHENWALD.*

It was a day of blue skies after a frosty night. The forest and the fields north of the town were bright with spring. The roadsides were lined with prisoners coming to town from the camp. No effective check had yet been placed on their free movement to prevent the spread of typhus and dysentery.

We scanned the files of men curiously. They did not seem very different from thousands of other refugees streaming westward these days. Many of them were thin to the point of emaciation and all were haggard and unshaven. Some wore striped prison suits and some civilian clothes much more ragged and dirty, with the coloured diamonds of cloth to indicate their nationality. Only once did I notice a man who looked out of the ordinary. He was very old. He had a long, yellow-white beard, and was walking alone, apparently deep in thought. Just as we passed him he stopped and crossed himself.

The approach to Buchenwald itself was impressive. On the left of the broad concrete highway, which swept up to the entrance lodge of the compound proper, was a large enclosure bounded by a double fence of electrified wire. Behind this, spread over many acres, were the shattered and blackened walls of the small-arms and ammunition factories in which many of the prisoners had been employed. A raid by the Royal Air Force in August 1944 destroyed the factories, but left the camp untouched.

The entrance lodge was a building of roughcast concrete and brown wood, surmounted by a squat tower and a flagpole from which hung limply a great black flag. The inner enclosure was again an irregular rectangle bounded by barbed and electrified wire supported on steel uprights. It extended over the crest of a ridge and down towards a swampy hollow. All round it were forests but every square foot of cleared land was commanded by high, rustic watchtowers where machine-guns and searchlights were mounted.

On one side of the driveway leading to the gates, half-a-dozen American soldiers stood guard over a pile of weapons taken from the guards the day before.

At first I had difficulty in obtaining permission to enter. A committee of doctors who had been inmates had just taken over control of the sick and had issued a quarantine order. Eventually, however, I was given a pass and someone went for a guide.

A French-speaking prisoner approached us. I asked him if he knew how many prisoners were still in camp and he said: 'We are told there are still 21 000. There were 57 000 here when I came.'

'What happened to the rest?' I asked.

'I think they are dead. Come, I will show you the places where they burned them.'

I said: 'Wait. They have gone for a doctor to guide us.'

It was hard to believe that the barracks, large though they were, could house 21 000 people. It was almost impossible to believe that they once housed 57 000, the population of a small city.

Some of the buildings were massively built of brick and concrete. The streets were either cobbled or paved. Farther down the hill one could see makeshift wooden structures like outsized fowlhouses.

The prisoners about the gates showed more signs of disease, hunger and distress than the men walking on the road from Weimar. They stood in the sunshine in groups, listlessly watching, coughing and scratching themselves. Some of them crowded around, smiling. They stank with the thin, sour smell of starvation.

A small man with blank, bright eyes came bustling up the hill. He said: 'I am Dr Hugo Mortelmans, a prisoner of this camp. I will be glad to guide you to whatever you wish to see. You will of course first wish to visit the crematorium.'

We walked towards a concrete building with tall black chimneys. It was enclosed by a high wall. Mortelmans told me he had been a lecturer in pathology at Antwerp University until taken by the Gestapo for resistance activity. He had been employed in the Waffen SS Department of Histology.

As we headed for the crematorium, a crowd tailed a long behind us. Mortelmans led the way up to an iron gate, pounded on it and spoke to a guard inside. Then he turned to the following crowd and told them to go away. 'They have a great curiosity to see the death-house — now,' he remarked dryly.

The iron gate opened and we stepped into an enclosed yard with cracked slabs of concrete and gravel. Piled neatly against one wall were 103 blue-white human corpses. They were naked. They were, almost without exception, the corpses of men who had been far gone in starvation and disease when death took them. Their skulls had been shaved. Many had been beaten. There were whip cuts on the skin of their backs and some were mottled purple with bruises. The bodies were spattered with dried blood and pus and dripped clear fluid from their orifices.

A motor truck with high sides had been backed up to the pile of corpses. Two men came out of the building and began loading the dead into the truck. One of the workers was a gnarled man with a black, stubbly beard and the other a fair boy of not more than twenty. Both were strong and well nourished.

The fair boy said he was Polish. His father and mother had died in this camp two years before. He had been put to work in the death-house because he was very strong and seemed immune to disease. They needed strong men to do the work here — regulars. He had been well fed.

He said all this without visible emotion. I looked hard at him in the light, and saw that his skin was clear and pink with health. He was very nearly fat.

He returned my regard quite impersonally. He and the gnarled man bent down again and they began lifting up the thin, paper-light corpses with a dexterous swing. Both of them grunted as they swung one body, different from the rest, on to the death-truck. He had been a large, heavily fleshed man. A bruise round his neck. His tongue projected.

Mortelmans said: 'That is the body of an SS guard. We caught some of them before they fled. This one hanged himself in his cell last night.'

We then went into the crematorium where six furnaces stood open. Each contained the blackened frames of what had once been men. Above the entrance door was a verse lettered in gold and black, beginning:

> *'Worms shall not devour but flames*
> *Consume this body. While I lived*
> *I always loved the heat and light...'*

Mortelmans said these furnaces had blazed, day and night, for years. Now we must see the execution yard where the gallows had stood, and the garrotting room.

The garrotting room was a basement fourteen feet by twenty feet, with whitewashed walls and a smooth cement floor. Two narrow, grated slits above ground level let in daylight. A row of electric light globes ran down the centre of the ceiling. On three walls, about seven feet from the floor, was a row of holes which had been imperfectly plastered up and covered, or partly covered, with limewash in a hasty effort at concealment. Mortelmans went to a bench and picked up a metal hook about nine inches long, and a small loop of windowsash cord. He explained that the method of execution was to place the cord round a man's neck and suspend him from the hook in the wall. He strangled to death. At busy times death was hastened by forcing other prisoners to grasp victims round the knees and bear down with their weight. Refractory victims, or those who showed signs of life after being taken down, had their skulls smashed with a club.

Somebody came up and thrust the club into my hands — a three-foot length of heavy wood with a shaped handle and knob to keep the grasp from slipping. It was something like a baseball bat. It had been used so much that the thick end was worn and shredded. It was stained with blood that showed, black and glistening, against the pale wood.

Mortelmans told me that he believed between twenty and thirty British and American airmen had been executed here a few months before.

'How many people do you estimate have been killed here?' I asked.

Mortelmans shook his head. 'I think they have destroyed the camp records,' he said. 'Perhaps no one will ever know for sure. Twenty thousand, thirty thousand, forty... No one will ever know for sure.'

A man with a hoarse, thick voice spoke in English: 'They were burning them day and night,' he said, 'for years.'

'Who are you?' I asked, looking at him. He was big with a heavy belly and red jowls. There were bluish veins in his nose and his small eyes were bloodshot.

'Me? I am an American citizen,' he said. 'I can prove it.'

'What are you doing here?'

'I have been here for thirteen years. I was a Communist. I come back to see my folks, my old pa and my old mam. They was German, see. I got sorta mixed up in it, and I never got out.'

'You managed to stay alive thirteen years in this place. How?'

'Plenty of us did. We took it easy. Me, I was chief electrician. I'm an electrician by trade. It's a big plant they got here. There's a lot to keep in order.'

'Did you know that camp commandant Koch I've heard about?' I asked.

'Ah,' he said softly, in his hoarse, thick voice, 'Koch, eh? What a sonofabitch he was! What a sonofabitch he was!'

'Did you see any of these executions?'

He shook his head. 'Only the stiffs afterwards, like you just seen.'

Climbing the stairs from the death-room, Mortelmans said against my ear: 'It is not yet safe to speak frankly here. Strange things have always gone on in this camp. Strange things are still going on.'

A hundred yards or so down the hill was the museum of pathology, a low, ugly building.

Mortelmans introduced Dr Mark Klein, professor of histology at the University of Strasbourg, who said that since his arrest a year before he had been employed in the small dissection room attached to the crematorium. He prepared sections and specimens of diseased tissue from cadavers. Klein showed us the collection of specimens in the laboratory anteroom, wearily and without comment — a collection of preserved dissections more varied and extensive than any I had hitherto seen in medical schools. I said: 'I don't know much about this sort of thing, Dr Klein, but it seems to me this work has been done with great skill and care. It has scientific value, I suppose?'

'Yes,' he said, 'it is beautiful work. We never lacked for material and choice. It has scientific value.'

'Would you say that the work done in this department as a whole had a scientific value?'

'Some had.'

'And the rest?'

'It was done to satisfy sadistic mania, the mania of those in control of this camp.'

I told him I had heard that workers in this department had, at the orders of Commandant Koch, preserved pieces of human skin bearing elaborate tattoo marks. Klein went into the laboratory and came out with four pieces of dried human skin each about ten inches square, and each bearing tattoo marks. He said that the man who made the collection had written a monograph on the subject, copies of which he had seen.

I asked if it were true that lampshades had been made and books bound with human leather. Personally, Klein replied, he had no knowledge of this, but the story that it had been done was current among prisoners.

A Polish laboratory assistant came forward and said that he had been working in the department for three years. He could swear to the fact that the wife of Commandant Koch had lampshades and bookbindings of human leather. Workers in dissecting rooms had strict instruction to preserve any good specimens of tattooing on cadavers. He could also swear that prisoners noted to have fine tattooing on their bodies were occasionally paraded for inspection before Koch and his wife.

'I will show you something else that they did,' he added.

He went to a wall cupboard and brought out two shrunken human heads mounted on wooden plinths. I looked at them carefully and said: 'These are anthropological specimens, aren't they? Jivaro work from South America?'

The assistant shook his head. 'If you look carefully, you will see that they are the heads of Eastern Europeans,' he replied. 'They were prepared by a technician who was interested to see if he could duplicate the Jivaro shrinking process.'

The heads were perfectly preserved and reduced. They seemed still to bear the expression with which the men died. The features were broad, coarsely Slavonic. Even hair and stubbled beard were preserved.

From the museum of pathology Mortelmans took us to Block 50, Waffen SS Department of Bacteriology and Serology, where Professor Maurice Suard, Angers Medical School, explained in detail the anti-typhus experiments conducted there. He stated that healthy prisoners had repeatedly been inoculated with the typhus virus and given various sera at various stages of the disease to observe the effect upon them. He also stated that execution by toxic injection was a method regularly used to get rid of surplus prisoners. The work done by the department had objective scientific value but it had been done with a complete disregard of human life and suffering.

Slave scientists had not been required to participate directly in experiments on human beings. Those had been conducted by Nazi doctors and technicians. Slave scientists had been used to prepare cultures and to do work in which there was more than ordinary danger of infection. The Germans had been almost ludicrously afraid of infection.

Suard then demonstrated the modern equipment with which the various laboratories and workrooms in the block were furnished. 'The work here was undertaken with the greatest consistency and orderliness,' he said. 'No expense was spared in the matter of equipment.'

From this point on, Dr Joseph Brau, physician of Coulommiers, France, took over as guide. He had been appointed chief physician of the volunteer medical staff who were tending prisoners until the American hospital teams could move in.

Brau was a slight, middle-aged man with serene eyes. In him I believe I detected the honesty of soul that can come only from self-conquest. He had seen everything. He was not afraid. He had not lost pity, but pity did not hinder him. It seemed, from the comments he made upon the things he showed me, that not love nor hate nor fear had power to blind him. He had the courage to admit that even such things as one saw here were part of the fabric of human life, therefore to be acknowledged without passion, but striven against without cease. Brau was the kind of man whose belief in a divine purpose was so profound that he had found tranquillity in the deepest pit of the earthly hell Hitler had created — the kind of tranquillity that needs no rest from the labour of living, no illusion of escape from the obliteration of dying.

'Here,' he said, 'I have really learned to work for men.' He said it with humility.

Down the hill of Buchenwald...past the barracks and the great communal laundry with its gleaming washing machines (for SS guards), and the great community kitchen with gleaming cookers (for SS guards). The cobbled pathways were swept and policed, and the air full of the sourness of death.

Brau's voice was quiet. 'I tell you there is no nationality in this thing. Some of my own countrymen behave like fiends. Here you could survive... Even if you were not valuable for your talents you could survive if you debased yourself. Some of those who have been here longest have suffered least... But the policy was directed towards the steady extermination of Jews and people from the east. If they could not work because they fell ill, or if they would not work or, if for the moment no work could be found for them, then they came down the hill. Once one started to come down the hill, it was the beginning of the end...

'Now these are the barracks of those who are well...'

Crowds of men were moving along the cobbled paths. They had no faces for me, except one — a man far gone in madness, with his mouth open, showing two long, white eyeteeth. He crouched in front of us, pointing to his mouth and stomach.

'*Vas-t'en,*' said Brau, sharply. The idiot leapt nimbly out of the way.

We went through a barbed-wire gate. Inside, they all wore striped clothing.

Out of the door of the barracks of those who were *well* came a strange figure, gangling and hopping. He wore only a striped jacket. His skull was unshaven, a yellow-white globe unsteadily balanced on a pole of a neck. The muscles on the lower part of his body had wasted away completely, even the great gluteus muscle. Tendons twitched like marionette wires under the loose skin. The legs were streaked and dripping with excrement. This creature leaned upon another who was only a little stronger than himself. Together they went down the hill.

Brau said: 'The difficulty of getting cases of advanced starvation back onto a nourishing diet will be very great...we have much trouble with diarrhoea and dysentery... For some time the death rate will not greatly diminish. There is too much to do...'

The floor of the barracks was puddled with filth. Men were lying or sitting in tiers of curved wooden bunks, their eyes gleamed in the half-darkness.

'Go through and inspect them,' said Brau. 'See? Ten men to a bunk where three might sleep and move with comfort. Space was very carefully rationed.'

As we began to walk down the corridor between the tiers of bunks a low, growling noise broke out. I did not recognise it as applause until someone started handclapping. A man crawled weakly out into the passage and stood to attention, saluting.

'English...ah, English, English!' Hands stretched out and touched us.

Somewhere, someone said, 'Hey, chum!! Chum. How are you, chum?'

I felt my arm lift up and my lips move, but I could not stop. I could not.

Brau's voice went on steadily. 'This man actually concealed his son here for three years... The child is five years old. See, he is not in too bad shape. The others fed him, a mouthful here and a mouthful there. We have about forty children registered already but this is the youngest. Recently all the children under ten or twelve years were taken away from new arrivals. We believe they were killed. Formerly it was only the girls who were killed. There are very few women in the camp, compared with numbers of men. We know that children of ten years have been used for the purposes of homosexuals. Cigarettes were the currency. We know, too, that among some of the prisoners there has been a traffic in human flesh cut from cadavers. Cigarettes were the currency...

'Now you must see the hospital.'

Down the hill. Just twenty paces down the hill. I cannot tell of that, only say that the dead still walked to stand in the sun, stark naked, shivering in uncontrollable rigours; that they lay in the filth of their diseases in the tiered bunks. I can only say that their voices were like the sound of wind in a dark, deep place; that the image of their eyes and their teeth as they smiled will, until the day I die, remain life's most terrible recollection.

I said to Brau: 'The only humane thing the Germans did here, they did when they strangled them.'

Brau replied: 'That is true.'

We did not go to the brothel kept by the guards for prisoners who had money or cigarettes; and to which women were assigned as final punishment. On the way through the vegetable garden kept by the prisoners for the tables of the privileged, I was ill. Brau said: 'This is the first time, then, that you have seen one of these places?'

'No,' I said, 'It is only the worst.'

I went back to the town where Goethe, Schiller and Liszt lived and worked.

Chapter 9

Buchenwald, Belsen, Dachau, Auschwitz — names that enraged the world too late.

I spent, in all, fourteen or fifteen days in concentration camps — not one-hundredth part of the time needed to learn the whole truth. Before the end of 1945 investigators for the War Crimes Commission spent an aggregate of months in concentration camps and still did not learn the whole truth.

I talked to men and women prisoners whom I could believe; and to men and women prisoners whom I could not believe. But some of whom I could believe told me of the experiments on prisoners in Dachau to determine the effects on the human body of prolonged immersion in ice-cold water. The object was ostensibly to discover the best treatment for German aircrews rescued from the North Sea.

A Belgian girl from Auschwitz told me it was the practice there to throw newborn infants alive into the crematorium furnaces; that her own child, conceived in rape by a German officer, had been taken from her and disposed of that way. I believed her.

A Polish officer from the same camp recounted how hundreds of Russian and Polish prisoners had been beaten and kicked to death by guards. He told me how his best friend fell into a latrine pit in the centre of a barracks hut, smothered there, and was left to rot because the inmates were too weak to pull him out. I believed him.

The stories mounted endlessly. Somewhere or other in the middle of the round, I stopped listening, seeing and feeling and began again to think. The visual image, the spoken word, no longer had power to nauseate and horrify. I had hardened. These things had happened. They were real. There could be no denial of them. They had happened on a scale beyond the compass of any one mind. Nothing could be done about them now. They would in time be listed, classified, analysed in an appalling indictment of an entire nation when confronted by irrefutable evidence of atrocity. The average German denied hysterically that he knew anything at all about it and in the same breath said that even if he had known there was nothing he could have done — nothing at all. Those interlocked excuses seemed to satisfy the individual German conscience.

The first reaction of American officers to the 'I did not know' attitude was cold disgust and rage.

After the discovery of the Ohrdruff camp on 6 April, Colonel Hayden Sears, of Boston, ordered every able-bodied male German in the nearby village to parade. He took them in trucks to the camp on Sunday morning, 8 April, ejected three women who had come because they had mistaken the terms of the order, and forced the others to inspect the rotting remains of thirty men clubbed and stabbed to death in a final orgy of murder before the guards fled. 'Come nearer and look at the nature of these wounds,' Sears ordered them.

He led them to an iron-roofed shed where forty more corpses were stacked and sprinkled with quicklime. Sears said: 'Look closely, you Germans. These men did not die of malnutrition. They were beaten to death. You have been brought here to see with your own eyes what is entirely reprehensible by any human standards. This is but a small part of the scenes we witness in Germany today. SS troopers have similarly murdered American prisoners. We hold the entire German nation responsible for such fiendish acts. The entire German nation supported and tolerated the Nazi Government. This shows why Americans cannot be your friends. All of you are responsible for this. Your names are being taken so that you can testify at the trials of the criminals directly responsible.'

Sears then addressed a German military surgeon who had been paraded with the party. 'Doctor,' he said, 'you will observe that these men have either been bludgeoned to death or stabbed in the jugular vein. Does this fit your conception of behaviour for a master race?'

The major replied: 'I cannot believe that Germans did this.'

An American medical officer also with the party interjected coldly: 'I presume your scientific mind still functions, Doctor. You observe that these men have been dead at least a week — several days before American troops got here. Who do you think, then, committed these murders?'

The German said in a voice so low it was scarcely audible: 'I would not have believed it, if I had not seen it with my own eyes.'

Two guards who had been captured trying to escape from the district were then brought forward to look at the bodies. What seemed extraordinary to me was the fact that neither of them looked brutal. Outwardly they were ordinary men. They were not even noticeably Teutonic in type; they were two ordinary-looking men, pale and sweating profusely with terror.

One cracked under the strain, burst into a whining hysteria of protest. 'I didn't do it! I did not commit these murders! I didn't know about these things! I didn't, I didn't, I didn't!' Tears streamed down his ashen cheeks.

The party then marched in complete and deathly silence back along the corpse-strewn path to the camp gates and was driven into a nearby pine forest where, in a clearing, was a burial trench three hundred yards long and twenty feet wide. To conserve space, an attempt had been made to burn the bodies on an improvised grille of railway rails over a furnace pit fed with sawn pine logs.

The great burial trench was almost filled with ash and human debris from which, here and there, emaciated limbs projected. Near the furnace were a dozen partly cremated bodies. A stench of roasted flesh and putrefaction filled the air.

Sears said to his interpreter: 'Tell them this was the fate of thousands, tens of thousands. Torture, beating, slow starvation, overwork. This. Make them stand closer. Make them look at the hooked poles for turning the roasting bodies. *Make them stand closer and look!*'

A paint merchant from the village detached himself from the group of now terrified Germans. 'The citizens of Ohrdruff were forbidden to come near this place,' he said. 'They did not know about this. This is the work of less then one per cent of Germans. The rest should not be held responsible.'

Sears replied: 'Germans supported a government which committed these crimes. The prisoners here were employed digging underground fortifications at Gotha. The German people accepted the use of this and other slave labour. Your guilt is plain to the world. Go to your homes, and remember what you have seen. Remember it always.'

Perhaps the citizens of Ohrdruff did not know what the camp and the forest held; but one man could not be paraded that morning to be shown proof. He was the burgomaster who had the night before, at Sears' direction, issued the order to muster the people. When they came for him in the morning he and his wife were found hanged by sashcord to hooks on the wall of their bedroom. Before they hanged themselves, they had slashed their wrists with razor blades, just to make certain.

The parade of the Ohrdruff villagers was the first of many such angry efforts to bring home to Germans realisation of their guilt. One thousand citizens of Weimar were marched to Buchenwald and relentlessly made to look on its horrors.

The American officers who enforced the 'treatment' did not make even a formal gesture of chivalry by excluding women. At the camp both men and women fainted or vomited or stood with their eyes tightly shut, until ordered harshly to open them and look. Others stood blockishly, submissive, unresponding. Again the burgomaster and his wife committed suicide — this time after the inspection.

The first German language newspapers issued by the Allied Military Government in Western Germany displayed photographs of piles of corpses and herds of emaciated prisoners. Pictorial posters were printed and tacked up on public noticeboards. The skyline of Buchenwald, the profile of the crematorium, the tiers of bunks in that terrible hospital hut labelled legibly, 'Section for Typhus', 'Section for Open Tuberculosis', 'Section for Diseases of the Bowels', and even, 'Section for Children and French Generals' became familiar to every town-dweller.

I do not think that this propaganda was, on the whole, psychologically effective. The Germans were in no condition for the lesson to sink in. Their cities lay in ruin and their countryside was being plundered by tens of thousands of escapees from all kinds of bondage from civilian and military gaols, prisoner-of-war compounds, concentration camps, or factories and farms to which they were assigned as slave labourers.

Why agonise over the suffering of Jews, Poles and Gypsies who died of starvation in their cages because the American and British 'terror fliers' had cut the roads and railways that carried their rations? German mothers and children in flight from burning cities died because fighter planes strafed every vehicle that moved. The wounded, soldiers and civilians alike, suffered the torment of amputations without anaesthetics because stocks were exhausted or destroyed by bombing. Why not print pictures of what tortures the Allies perpetrated?

When a film of Belsen was screened in one north German POW centre, its Wehrmacht inmates whistled and stamped and shouted: 'What about the Indian famines? What about the Congo miners?'

Early propaganda to induce guilt was mistimed and failed entirely to convey the fact that concentration camp prisoners had been systematically tortured and murdered for more than ten years. Torture and murder were the means by which the Nazis silenced all protest within the Third Reich.

Berlin, 1945
Photograph: Osmar White

Part IV

THE
AFTERMATH

Chapter 10

Long before Allied troops reached the big concentration camps in which death squads specialised in the extermination of Jews and Slavs, and the world learned the meaning of Hitler's promise to arrive at 'a final solution', the fighting men who stormed into Germany were angry and in vengeful mood. They had learned in France and Belgium, at first hand, of Nazi atrocities; of the mass execution of hostages, senseless burnings and beatings, sadistic interrogation of men and women suspected of supporting resistance cells. Few wavered in the conviction that the Germans they killed deserved their fate, or that the survivors had little right to humane consideration. Thus, at first the treatment of German civilians was harsh. Eisenhower's broadcast proclamation — 'WE COME AS CONQUERORS' — implied the right of military commanders to requisition whatever accommodation remained intact in half-demolished towns. The aged, the sick, the very young, were often driven out into the ruins to fend for themselves.

'The only way to teach these krauts war doesn't pay is to kick them about the way they kick other people about.'

I heard that idea expressed time and again. Conquest tacitly implied the right to booty. The victorious troops appropriated whatever portable enemy property they fancied — liquor and cigars, cameras, binoculars, shotguns and sporting rifles, ceremonial swords and daggers, silver ornaments and plate, and fur garments.

This sort of petty looting was known as 'liberating' or 'souveniring'. Military police looked the other way until the more rapacious liberators, usually support and transport personnel, began to steal expensive motor cars, antique furniture, radio sets, machine tools and other industrial equipment, and devise ingenious means of smuggling the stolen property to the coast from which small craft could ferry it to England. Only after looting became an organised criminal racket when the fighting ceased, did the Military Government step in and enforce the law. Until then the soldiers took what they wanted and often kicked Germans about in doing it.

Yet I saw few cases of calculated or depraved brutality. The troops felt that they were only handing out rough justice, morally valid retribution, to a race whose armies had plundered Western Europe for nearly five years.

Far from modifying the invaders' behaviour, the submissiveness of German civilians made them more contemptuous and angry. One of the few times I saw American soldiers deliberately and soberly smash up a German house was at Erfurt. The occupants had fled, leaving a note in the kitchen which read: 'THIS IS THE HOME OF PEOPLES LIKE YOU — DO NOT BREAK IT IF YOU PLEASE.'

There were numerous such notes left in abandoned German houses. They did not always evoke indignation like that of the infantrymen clearing Erfurt. They certainly did not have the effect the writers intended.

After the fighting moved on to German soil there was a good deal of rape by combat troops and those immediately following them. The incidence varied between unit and unit according to the attitude of the commanding officer. In some cases offenders were identified, tried by court martial, and punished. The army legal branch was reticent, but admitted that for brutal or perverted sexual offences against German women, some soldiers had been shot — particularly if they happened to be Negroes. Yet I know for a fact that many women were raped by white Americans. No action was taken against the culprits. In one sector a report went round that a certain very distinguished army commander had made the wisecrack: 'Copulation without conversation does not constitute fraternisation.'

A divisional officer once remarked dryly during a discussion on the non-fraternisation edict: 'This is surely the first time in history a serious effort has been made to deny soldiers the use of the women in a country they have conquered!'

Probably the most objective and credible account of the situation was given by an intelligent, middle-aged Austrian woman in Bad Homburg. 'Yes, of course the soldiers take women,' she said. 'After the occupation of this place we were troubled for many nights by soldiers coming to the doors and asking for *Fräulein*. Sometimes they forced their way into the houses with kicks and blows. Sometimes the women hid, or escaped.'

I asked her if she knew if the women were actually taken with violence. She thought for a while and replied: 'No. I don't think it often happens like that. Except where soldiers are in a gang. You must remember that your German women these days have not the horror of being taken violently by a man that they had before the Nazis spread their beliefs. They are frightened — yes. But they are more frightened of getting beaten than they are of getting taken by force. You will see. If your soldiers are patient they will not find German women unobliging.'

What happened was not hard to envisage. A few, drunken rowdies in a dark street and '*Kommen Sie hier, Fräulein!*'

Most of the Third Army correspondents whose job took them to the front suffered at one time or another from what the medics cheerfully called 'jeep disease'. Jeep disease was anything that went wrong with the human body as a result of being jounced ten or twelve hours at a stretch, day after day, on roads cut to pieces by tank and gun tracks. If a man developed floating kidneys or piles or lumbago it was jeep disease. If, in snowy weather, he complained of seeing men on horseback and statues that weren't there, it was jeep disease, too.

One particular morning I was riding with a PFC from the press transport pool known affectionately as Charlie the Demon Driver. He was expert at negotiating obstacle courses in record time. When cutting in and out of truck convoys with Charlie at the wheel it was advisable to close one's eyes and keep them closed, taking only an occasional peep at the laxative hazards ahead.

I took a peep and saw a man on the roadside. He was enormous — well over six feet tall. He had an enormous black beard and an even more enormous astrakhan hat. He wore a long, ragged greatcoat with a broad belt and crossed bandoliers. He was standing beside a wheelbarrow on which were stacked a red-striped feather mattress, an assortment of tins and bundles, and a coop with two live chickens in it. As we passed him, throwing up a spray of slush, he neither flinched nor drew back. He smiled. His teeth shone in his beard. His eyes rolled. He threw us a salute to end all salutes.

Charlie cut in front of a three-tonner and roared on round the bend. I did not even have time to look back. I sat thinking for a while. Then I asked, confidentially, leaning over, 'Charlie, did you see anything on the roadside back there?'

Charlie's lantern jaw worked steadily at his gum. 'Uh? What do you mean anything?'

'A man with a black beard, for instance?'

For five seconds he said nothing, then: 'Russki. There'll be a heap of Russkies coming out from now on. Just the first, I guess.'

Just the first... Soon, every day for months, a procession of liberated slaves was commonplace on every country road in Germany.

They came in knots and files through the spring rain, marching in the long grass or on the shoulders of the roads. In the early days one often saw their mutilated bodies where they had trodden on S mines at the approaches to culverts and bridges. But they did not delay. They were free, so they marched — marched anywhere as long as it was out.

The firstcomers were the farm workers. They looked strong and well-enough fed. They wore the rags of all the uniforms of Europe. Some had boots, some clogs, some the gaping wrecks of shoes. Some went barefoot even in the frost, others wrapped their feet in blanket strips and sacking. They were marked by this kind of poverty but they were not in bad physical shape.

Many really marched, in columns of three. At the beginning of the day they trudged along with a swing and when tanks thundered up they grinned and waved and saluted. The tank crews bound up the line waved back until their arms ached. At first they threw down packets of cigarettes and spare K rations, but very soon there were too many eager hands.

By the end of the day the marchers were less cocky. They did not wave so much and shambled along in loose order. There was no shelter in the villages. They made camps under blown bridges or in forest clearings where at night one could see them crouched over smoky fires.

As the armies went deeper into Germany the character of the marchers began to change. The processions no longer comprised vigorous — or comparatively vigorous — men. Some limped and were obviously ill and half-starved. Women and children were among them. The older women had weather-beaten faces and sullen eyes, but the girls gave their liberators gap-toothed smiles. Nearly everyone had a handcart or a baby carriage piled with loot.

Generally speaking, these first slave workers to be freed in the Rhineland displayed no particular personal bitterness against their masters. Even eastern Europeans seemed to have been treated humanely, or at least as valuable farm animals. I recall vividly one old peasant woman who came out to the commander of a reconnaissance column near Besignheim and begged him to stop her Russian from running away. Her son and husband, she said, had been taken for the Wehrmacht, and without her Russian there would be nobody left to do the heavy work about the farm.

There would be nobody to plough and sow. In the winter they would all starve.

We had a look at the Russian. He was a lumpy, silent youngster with an expression of subnormal good humour but he was quite determined to run away. He had his bundle of clothes. The old woman had apparently been following him along the road, remonstrating with him.

The tank commander said something unprintable and signalled the column on. When I last saw the queer pair, the woman was sitting in the ditch with her head in her hands, and the Russian was striding purposefully away.

One of the first Frenchmen I encountered was a cheerful, red-nosed villain from Marseilles. He was leading a little group of compatriots down the riverside road between Wittlich and Trier. He wore his ragged coat like a cape, and flourished an ash plant as a baton of office.

True, true, he declaimed, the accursed Boche had seized him, wrenched him from the arms of his loving wife and little ones in the month of August 1940. In all that time he had received no word, no word at all of Madame Lebrun. Yet to tell the truth, the Boche in this part of the world were not such bad people. When all the foreign workers had been herded out of Trier on the approach of the Americans he had been forced to go along with them. But he had been clever — they had not taken him across the Rhine. Emil Lebrun had not been born yesterday. Ah, indeed no! Once across the Rhine a man was finished. He escaped that fate. How? Why, he simply ignored Boche orders. He had concealed himself in a cellar. There was a woman, of course — a farm woman who fed him in the haystack where he lay hidden when the Germans were retreating. No, in truth, not all Boches were monsters ... For himself, it had been endurable. He had been employed as a cellarman in one of the great wine caves at Trier. Would I be interested, now, in exchanging a lift for him and his comrades for a little useful information?

Being outward-bound I declined regretfully. The followers of the red-nosed cellarman looked discouraged.

One man stood apart from the rest, looking placidly into the distance. He was young and had a smooth, brown face. I asked if he, too, were French. The cellarman said in a discreet undertone that he was an officer, Lieutenant Raoul de Valbray. Sometimes he became almost insane with anxiety to get home; other times he was just abstracted, as at present. Poor fellow, he had had a bad head wound and it had left him moody.

Now he was going back to his parents' house in Saint Lo. Was it true that Saint Lo was quite destroyed?

My first impressions of the Nazi forced-labour system in the Rhineland lacked evidence that the workers had been brutally mistreated. They had been fed, housed and provided with basic necessities. Some hardly resented their slavery. Half-a-dozen Frenchmen employed at the press camp at Idar Oberstein had, for the whole four years of their forced labour, been servants in German hotels. They were frank. Except for air raids they'd had an easy time. Pay was poor, admittedly, but what was pay when there was nothing in the shops to buy anyway? They'd had enough to eat and plenty of diversion with German women, who were vigorous and suffered much from the manpower shortage. Having no particular family ties, they did not want to go home at all. Now that Germany was a conquered country it should be amusing for an enterprising Frenchman!

But after the Rhine crossings and the fall of the industrial cities, the stories and the appearance of the wayside vagrants began to change. One heard tales of merciless slave-driving in bomb-battered factories, of an eighty-hour working week, of starvation and bitter cold and monotony, and indignities maliciously contrived by arrogant overseers. One heard tales of nightmarish rail journeys in closed cattle trucks with the floors ankle-deep in human excrement and in which the weaker conscripts died of fatigue, cold and suffocation.

On the roads the streams of vagrants thickened, and were joined by the very old and the very young.

When the Wehrmacht withdrew from an area, or grouped to await a chance to surrender en masse, as they did in the last days of the war, the liberated hordes appropriated every wheeled vehicle they could find — even oxcarts drawn by milch cows if the oxen could not be found. There were farm carts, milk floats, bakers' waggons, buggies, sometimes drawn by skinny horses but more often by teams of men and women. Once I saw an ancient steamroller, belching smoke and sparks, towing a long line of drays and carts on the Berlin–Frankfurt autobahn.

These processions were amazing and ludicrous, but rarely did I hear a soldier laugh at them. The fantasy, the sheer improbability of this vast migration of homeless people was too heavily salted with suffering.

As the weeks passed the obvious camping sites in forests or on roadside flats became clogged and reeking with accumulated filth. The hunger of the vagrants became more savage and demanding as the latecomers travelled through 'eaten out' country. Later still, bands of conscript workers and POWs were joined by thousands of prisoners escaped from concentration camps — men and women carrying with them all the diseases of the years of enforced degradation and starvation. They crawled with lice and fleas. Some were so emaciated and weak that they did not get far. They died and their companions buried them in shallow graves marked by a stake with a truss of straw tied on as a crosspiece.

Lives also began on the road. One morning I stopped to talk with a band of Latvian workers travelling west from Apolda. They had with them a woman wearing a ragged, bloodstained skirt. She staggered along, supported by one of the men who carried a bundle in the crook of his free arm. I asked him what was wrong with her. He replied that she had given birth to a child during the night — in a clearing without shelter, of course. Where else? Here was the child, a boy. It was wrapped in a piece of window curtain — a withered, blue-faced, simian scrap making thin, mewing noises.

The mother was a strong girl, the man assured me. She would survive. She could rest when they reached the next town.

Later we met a couple travelling apart from the main group. A husky fellow in a green uniform jacket was pushing a large handcart loaded with household goods plundered from some farmhouse. On top of the load a young woman sprawled, resting. It was unusual to see a comely female among these wretched, travel-weary people, but this girl was a beauty. Her face was deeply tanned but unmarred by lines of strain or hunger. Her hair was black and glossy and her body under a cotton bodice and dirndl was slim and firm. As we passed she flashed me a smile that revealed even, blue-white teeth. She was, I think, one of the few — the very few — to whom the freedom road was only an adventure. She had that kind of face. She was not the sort of woman who suffers in a male world.

After the cessation of hostilities in May, the Displaced Persons Division of Allied Military Government in Frankfurt estimated that the number of homeless foreigners in Germany exceeded five million. Later in Berlin, Dr Ferdinand Friedensburg, Director of the German Institute of Economic Research, told me that about ten million foreign workers had been employed in the Reich. [White's full discussion of slave labour in Nazi Germany is provided in Appendix III.]

As far as I could discover, neither the American nor British authorities made any adequate plans to provide subsistence for these foreign workers or organise their repatriation after the cessation of hostilities in May. The totality of the German collapse took the invaders by surprise. They had expected that basic civil administration would continue to function and were nonplussed when it fell apart.

Most Nazi municipal officials and police had abandoned their posts and fled in fear of their lives. In only one town, Jena, did I actually witness a clash between DPs and local police. The tank crews ahead of the main American column had made the police surrender their firearms, but the infantry did not arrive until next day and in the meantime the Germans rearmed themselves with bicycle tyre tubes loaded with lead washers. They charged a mob of Frenchman and Poles plundering a bakeshop in a narrow street. Things looked bad for the looters until several jeeploads of American officers and correspondents, who were looking the town over, saw what was going on and drove the police back to their marshy barracks at pistol point. One Pole lay in the gutter with his head split open. A Frenchman with a broken collarbone leant against a lamppost, cursing and spitting out teeth and blood.

Their comrades ignored the injured men, took a savage kick or two at the behinds of the retreating police, and then returned gleefully to handing out loaves of greyish, potato-flour bread through the smashed windows of the bakery.

Just as we were about to move on a pigtailed girl came racing round the corner, stopped when she saw the jeeps and cried shrilly, 'Come quickly! Come quickly, please! The Poles have broken into the wineshop. They are drinking all the wine!' She was an ugly little girl with a pasty face and blue popeyes.

A captain in the leading jeep put his pistol back in its hoist and asked, 'What does she want?'

'She says the Poles are looting a wineshop,' I said.

He thought for moment, looking at the unconscious man in the gutter, the Frenchman hawking and retching, and the crowd laughing and shouting and scrambling for loaves.

'Better ask her where the wineshop is,' he said. 'We might get there in time to liberate a bottle or two ourselves.'

I told the child not to worry about the wineshop, to go home and stay off the streets. She looked at me blankly for a moment, then her popeyes misted with tears and she ran off.

Two or three blocks further downtown I pulled up to question another group of foreign workers who were watching German civilians queued up to surrender their shotguns and cameras to the burgomaster's pool. Most were French and their stories were unremarkable. They had been conscripted in 1943 and sent to work in various small plants connected with the optical industry. A hard life but what could one expect of the Boche? Now they were going home. They would start as soon as they could get enough food and equipment to see them on their way.

These workers were poorly clad but, for DPs, they looked remarkably clean. Several were freshly shaven and had slicked down their hair. They talked with animation, laughed, asked about their home towns, and how things were with France.

They looked better off than most of their kind but I thought it probable one or two of them could do with a meal. In the back of the jeep was a carton containing C ration cans. I leaned back casually and handed out two or three to the hungriest looking of the group. In seconds the jeep was the centre of a milling, growling mob. The laughing, gesticulating men were transformed into feral animals with pinched faces and clawing, pleading hands. 'Please, please, monsieur…and I…and I… For the love of God, monsieur! I!'

The driver let in the clutch and we cut through them. The C rations were gone in half a minute, a half-minute of realisation that left my face sweaty and my stomach knotted with shock.

Military government units moved into populated areas as soon as the fighting ceased and they were able, despite the flight of the people who had exerted civil authority, to establish a semblance of order and begin to restore essential services. But when the slave labourers and POWs started to clog the roads in uncounted thousands, looting their way from town to town and village to village, the situation became impossible to control.

Only a small proportion of those who broke out of camps or left the districts to which they had been drafted with the intention of making their own way home succeeded in doing so. They ended up in hastily established refugee centres, barely surviving on starvation rations requisitioned from already inadequate civilian food stocks and living in conditions of indescribable squalor. Elements among the survivors of the big concentration camps often banded together to reap a harvest of vengeance on German people who so strenuously denied all knowledge of Nazi atrocities. Sparsely populated areas, until then spared the horrors of war, often suffered grievously at the hands of these criminal gangs.

I remember vividly one miserable hamlet on the Fulda River where I was shown the battered and violated bodies of two children, aged seven and twelve, victims of liquor-maddened Russians who had slaved in the deep salt mines for three years.

Chapter 11

By the end of April the dismemberment of Germany was complete. The forces commanded by Simpson and Hodges had sealed off the Ruhr and after more than two weeks of bitter fighting forced the surrender of Model's entire army group, the remnants of 35 divisions totalling more than 350 000 men. The British under Montgomery advanced almost unopposed across the north German plain through Rhine, Osnabruck and Munster to the outskirts of Bremen and Hamburg. In the centre and south, Patton's and Patch's armour thundered on to and beyond the Elbe, forward elements penetrating Czechoslovakia as far as Pilsen before orders from SHAEF halted the advance for reasons no one at the front then understood. The roads to Berlin and Prague stood open. Why pause?

The mere occupation of German territory was no longer news. I needed a more comprehensive picture of events than I could get while caught up in the little whirlpools of collapse and capitulation.

On 23 April I returned to SHAEF headquarters at the Hotel Scribe in Paris and heard the news that the Russians had entered Berlin and were shelling the Reichschancellery. An announcement of unconditional surrender was expected at any minute. But where and how and by whom? Nobody knew. The top brass were playing very close to the chest. In the briefing room nothing much had changed except the position of the flags on the great wall maps.

Crazy headlines in crazy French newspapers: *Germany surrenders*. Germany will not surrender... *Hitler dead*. Hitler fled. *Peace*. No peace... *Incidents on the Elbe*. All quiet on the Elbe...

Tension mounted. The harsh triple honking of the buzzers in the lobby announcing the imminence of a press release became more frequent. The three American news services hired nimble French youths to race from the briefing room to the dispatching office on the first floor with 'flashes'. Bets were made on who would score a two-second 'beat'. An officer of field rank solemnly started these absurd races with a barked 'Go!'.

25 April. Hitler escapes. Hitler killed.

1 May. Hamburg surrenders. Grand Admiral Doenitz broadcasts, 'I am Führer. I will continue to fight the British and Americans for as long as they hinder me in my fight against Bolshevism.'

4 May. Montgomery has crossed the Lower Elbe and beaten the Red Army to the occupation of Schleswig-Holstein and Denmark.

5 May. Yesterday Admiral von Friedburg surrendered all German forces in the north-west to Montgomery in his headquarters on Luneburg Heath.

Any minute now...

I had a friend in court at SHAEF — a master sergeant in army public relations with whom I had spent convivial evenings during the winter freeze in a little black-market restaurant off the Rue du Faubourg St Honoré where the proprietor served superbly camouflaged horse steaks with vintage Chateau Latour to wash them down. On the afternoon of 5 May the convivial sergeant, whose sources of information had consistently proved more reliable than those of his colonel, took me aside at the dispatch desk and muttered out of the corner of his mouth: 'This is it, buster. No announcement here, but there's a Dakota readied for the press. Strictly limited. Agencies and national reps only. Get weaving and remind them Australia's been fighting this f---king war, too. I never told you, but the party's at Rheims in the technical school where the boss has his set-up these days. There'll be a bus leaving for the airfield in an hour. Keep buttoned up or you'll get killed in the rush.'

L'Ecole Professionelle, Rheims, was a drab, commonplace French school crouching in a drab, grey twilight through which a light rain drifted.

On the wall of the anteroom, where sixteen witnesses for the world's press and radio networks waited for six hours while the last talks about protocol and procedure dragged on, hung a large-scale map of Europe. The coloured flags with which it once was sprigged had been taken out and arranged in a V at the bottom right-hand corner.

It was a fascinating map. A study of it offered me escape from the near intolerable tension of waiting. In time its contrasting tints merged and it assumed a likeness of forests and fields and rivers and lakes and mountains. Men moved on its roads and railways and canals. In my mind it became Europe itself — hung up on a schoolroom wall.

Two thousand and seventy-six days of war, waged with a ferocity unparalleled in history, had cut across this segment of the globe a swathe of ruin and misery a thousand miles long and six hundred miles deep. The fat, hatched blots were the bomb-pocked skeletons of cities. In them, and in the neglected farms, and charred woodlands, the dead were numbered in millions; and the homeless and hopeless, maimed and hungry, in scores of millions. Berlin, Warsaw, Budapest, Hamburg, Rostov, Cologne, Kiev, Breslau, Bremen, Odessa, Dresden — wherever the finger fell randomly, close by lay a city disembowelled. Brussels, Belgrade, Leningrad, Rotterdam, The Hague, Antwerp, Milan, Genoa — all mauled and stinking.

Here the Dutch were gathering their rags about them and starving with dull dignity. Here the half-exterminated Poles were plotting bitterly against one another for title to bankrupt estates and threadbare privileges. Here the cold-eyed Norwegians were watching the disquiet of their oppressors grow into panic as the spring days lengthened. Here on the Elbe, east of midnight, guns were still thundering and men dying as Hitler's Germany, like a snake beaten to a pulp, even now in the last minutes of its life, wriggled under the blows of weary and disgusted executioners.

Just before 2 am an officer of the Public Relations Division summoned us. We followed him up a flight of bare stone stairs down a narrow corridor and into a classroom which Eisenhower's staff had been using for briefings. It was forty feet long and thirty feet wide. The ceiling was white and the walls a faded blue. A long table stood in front of a flagged map of the battlefronts. The top of the table had been painted black and about it were set fifteen yellow deal chairs with unpadded seats. The table was furnished with thirteen pads of white notepaper, thirteen yellow pencils and six white inkpots. Nothing else.

We lined up against one wall behind a chalk line beyond which we were forbidden to walk until the signatories to the Act of Surrender were seated.

Black cables of sound recording gear and cinecameras coiled over the shabby, patterned carpet that covered most of the floor. A calendar on the wall behind the table read:

MONDAY
MAY 7
1945

Camera crews and sound technicians raced about, bent double, checking and re-checking their equipment. Staff officers paced up and down, glancing every few seconds at their wristwatches.

At 2.19 a British colonel walked in and said in a brisk voice: 'Get ready, gentlemen, they're coming.'

There was an echo of footsteps in the corridor and the Allied delegation, led by Admiral Sir Harold Burrough, walked in — all except the Frenchman, General Francois Sevez and Lieutenant-General Bedell Smith, Eisenhower's Chief of Staff and chief signatory for the Western Allies. As they entered the floodlights came on with a hiss.

Burrough and the Soviet delegates, Major General Suslapatov and Colonel Zikovitch, were the only men upon whom the cracking nervous strain of the last few days and hours seemed to have left no impression. Burrough's high-boned face was ruddy and gleaming. Suslapatov, a huge-shouldered giant of a man, filled his tight-waisted Russian jacket and striped whipcord breeches with a sort of bounding physical defiance of the room's weighted tensions. His gold teeth gleamed as he made casual asides to his aide. All the others had violet shadows under their eyes and their faces were pallid and slack.

Five minutes later Sevez hurried in, bowed to the table and shook hands nervously with his nearest neighbour. Then came Bedell Smith. He was never a robust-looking man but under the glare of the kleigs he looked ghastly, ill and exhausted.

All stood a little stiffly behind the chairs awaiting the Germans. The heat from the lights mounted steadily and we began to sweat.

At exactly 2.39 am the new chief of the German General Staff, Colonel General Jodl and General Admiral Hans von Friedeburg arrived — scraggy men in uniforms that had known wear. Both were fair-haired, fading to grey, both a little bald. They were accompanied by aides who were freshly shaven and brushed, their skins a pale pink and their eyes glassy through lack of sleep.

Jodl and von Friedeburg walked with rapid, nervous strides to the table. For a moment they stood to attention until Bedell Smith, with a slight acknowledging bow, motioned them to take the seats opposite him. They sat abruptly and Bedell Smith asked them in a low, scarcely audible voice if they fully understood the terms of the documents to be signed. A tall British interpreter leaned over and repeated the question in German. They murmured assent.

There was a momentary delay while Bedell Smith consulted his neighbours on some detail of procedure. Jodl restlessly tapped his fingers on the table. Then the hush exploded into a flurry of furtive movement as the documents were distributed.

Each was in quadruplicate, and every copy was signed by the naval, land and air authorities of the signatory Powers.

The film cameras made a low, whirring sound and dozens of small flash-globes popped as the official photographers, still bent double scuttled from point to point, ripping black papers from film packs and adjusting lenses. Every gesture, every muscle twitch was recorded. Pen nibs moved swiftly as aides passed copy after copy.

Air Marshal Robb, the RAF delegate, was the only man at the table who did not watch every movement of the signing. He appeared distracted, studying maps on the wall. The Russians were the only ones upon whose countenances could be discerned the faintest expression of satisfaction. They sat absolutely motionless and upright, chests out. Their slightly slanted eyes were narrowed and fixed unwinkingly on the Germans' hands.

Suddenly it was finished. Bedell Smith made a quick movement, delivered the first written orders of the Allied Commander-in-Chief to the surrendered forces of the Third Reich. Jodl said something inaudible to the British interpreter, who translated with startling loudness: 'He asks permission to say a few words.'

The American inclined his head. Jodl rose, leaned slightly forward over the table, the tips of his fingers pressed hard against its top. He said in German, in a low monotone: 'General, with this signature, the German people and the German armed forces are for better or for worse delivered into the hands of the victors. In this war, which has lasted for more than five years, both have achieved and suffered more, perhaps, than any other people in the world. In this hour I can only express the hope that the victors will treat them with generosity.'

The Germans then rose and walked quickly from the room. Jodl's eyes were suffused with tears and his face was etched with lines of bitter humiliation and despair. Von Friedeburg was less visibly affected. The Allied delegation followed in pairs, talking in low voices. Suslapatov's gold teeth were gleaming again.

The lights fizzed down and the cameramen wiped the sweat out of their eyes and mopped their foreheads.

'The press will follow me,' said General Frank Allen, chief of SHAEF's public relations division. Dutifully we followed him and dutifully crowded into a narrow corridor to watch the Germans pay their formal call on Eisenhower, seated behind an elaborate little desk on which miniature flags of the United Nations were draped. We heard him record his short victory speech in a quiet, clear, tired voice. His eyes, too, were purple-shadowed and his cheeks hung slackly.

That was how they made peace in Europe.

Chapter 12

Berlin, 3 July 1945.

That day storms swept over the city. Torrents of silver rain fell out of a wild sky. Thunder rolled. Water cascaded from shattered walls and flooded, broken pavements. Those pitiful, stripped sticks, the Tiergarten's trees, wept with it.

I stood in the lee of the Brandenburger Tor. It was decked with sodden red flags, but the stones of the arch were so pitted by shrapnel that its outline was hazy. On all sides the vista was one of ruin — ruin beyond belief. The metal dome of the Reichstag had run like tinsel in a match flame, exposing its warped supports. But the bronze eagles in their niches on the facade of the Reichschancellery still stood and screamed dumbly. Was there some portent in the fact that 66 000 tons of bombs had not destroyed them?

No. That was a morbid fear. The beast was for all time sealed in his lair — buried somewhere under a mountain of malodorous refuse screened by a tottering wall.

The winds that blew down the mazy, rubble canyons that had once been gracious thoroughfares were heavy with the stench of quenched fire and stale death. Uncounted corpses lay rotting under the wreckage, crushed or burned or entombed in cellars and sewers. Yet this macabre burial ground still teemed with life. Four million human beings were existing in it like vermin in a garbage tip. They hurried from fissure to fissure, crouching in the wind and rain. Or they toiled like ants made sluggish by the onset of winter, clearing debris from choked streets, handing from one to the other buckets filled with pulverised concrete and bricks, smashed glass and fragments of metal.

At the end of a working shift they huddled together or formed queues waiting for a handout of bread or potatoes, of bluish, watered milk if they had children with them — the payment for a day of labour. Most of them were women or old men with grey, furrowed faces and rheumy eyes.

Yes. This, the Brandenburger Tor, was the last milestone on the conquerors' road. There was no signpost pointing to a road beyond.

Long before the Red Army crushed pockets of suicidal resistance in Berlin, the British and American forces halted their virtually unopposed advance eastward and were under orders to withdraw behind the River Elbe from any areas they had occupied after crossing it.

Officers of the 4th Armored Division were bitterly vociferous in expressing their indignation. Time and again since the breakout from the Normandy beachheads, they claimed, Eisenhower had caved in to political pressures and held Patton back from exploiting the tactical successes he had won.

The old speculation persisted that Eisenhower, under orders from Roosevelt, had agreed to let Montgomery hog the limelight in showpiece campaigns along the Lower Rhine. Limey morale was low at home and needed a boost; and Uncle Sam needed Limey support for the next job in hand — which was to kick the shit out of the Commies! Now the Nazis were put down, the next army to whip was Communism. It was elementary commonsense to hit the Russians before they had a chance to recover from the exhaustion of their race to Berlin and a phoney propaganda victory. The Russkis had come to the end of their tether. They were scraping the bottom of the barrel for the dregs of their military manpower. Hit the sons of bitches now! It would save a heap of trouble later...

A less fanciful and cynical rationalisation was that Eisenhower had again been overcautious and decided to concentrate and conserve his forces to deal with the situation if the SS attempted to make a last stand in the Bavarian Redoubt.

The real reason for the halt on the Elbe was not known until the end of the year when censorship was relaxed and the world learned how Stalin had outsmarted his allies-of-convenience by reneging on agreements made at the Yalta and Potsdam conferences.

In the last days of June word came down the line that, under pressure from Washington and London, the Russians had agreed to share the occupation of Berlin with the British and Americans. It was poor recompense for the humiliation of being kept waiting for six weeks, but some consolation that Churchill and Truman had at last shown the guts to put Stalin in his place.

Crack regiments were chosen to put on a show of strength — enough strength to make the arrogant Reds think again and give them a bloody nose if they tried to muscle in on more territory. Patton was rumoured to be hopping mad and spoiling for a fight.

On 1 July a convoy of eighty press jeeps carrying more than two hundred correspondents set out ahead of the troops and arrived in the capital by midmorning. The journey was enlivened by a completely unexpected encounter with the advance guard of the Red Army moving up to replace the Americans in Thuringia. The armoured vehicles and guns of the Western Allies, immaculate in coats of fresh paint, rumbled along at parade-ground intervals.

Battle-shabby uniforms has been smartened up, boots polished and badges burnished. All ranks wore the ribbons of decorations and campaign medals.

Compared with these spruce columns converging on the city from west and north-west, the outbound Russians were a rabble. Their padded cotton jackets were grease-stained and threadbare, their transport a hodgepodge of antiquated trucks and horse-drawn waggons piled with looted furniture, and more than half of them travelled on foot. They marched beside the autobahn, shepherded by NCOs on tyreless German bicycles. Even the famed Russian artillery pieces were practically invisible under layers of dried mud.

A British correspondent travelling beside me said with near awe in his voice: 'Good God, so these are the chappies who slogged all the way from Stalingrad, beating the blazes out of the Jerries all the way!'

These were, indeed, the men of the armies which had fought and beaten two-thirds of Germany's land forces on the Eastern Front while the magnificently equipped British and Americans had trouble enough dealing with the other third in Normandy, Italy and along the Siegfried Line. They were stocky, hard-faced peasants and herdsmen from the Steppes. They looked inured to hardship and utterly indifferent to the show of mechanised might put on to impress them. Perhaps, I thought, mere machines of war could never in the long run prevail against a peasant truly determined to resist foreign invaders of their homeland. But then the atom bombs had yet to burst over Hiroshima and Nagasaki.

I was assigned a billet in an apartment house near the Zehlendorf West railway station, slept for an hour, and then took a jeep down the Potsdammerstrasse into the city. Its outer suburbs had escaped obliteration. Some streets were almost unscarred, but British bombs and Russian shells had eviscerated the metropolis proper.

From high points only vast expanses of debris could be seen — skeletons of buildings, an infinitely complicated honeycomb of tall, roofless walls. The Russian estimate that four million people still survived in these ruins seemed incredible — until one remembered that survival is possible on a bare minimum of water, food and warmth.

Not one Berliner in a hundred was getting more than the bare minimum. They continued to exist in a state of catatonic shock which submerged all normal reactions to the disaster that had befallen them. Families stayed together by accident of proximity — or were dispersed by accident of dispersal. No one thought of tomorrow. They lived only from hour to hour. The past and the future were equally unreal. Relationships, except between mothers and young children, counted for nothing. The death of adult relatives or friends was an event of such little significance that it scarcely called for comment. One buried the bodies in the garden if they died nearby. There was no transport to take them to a cemetery. If they died elsewhere — so much the better. Someone else would have the trouble of digging a grave.

It was a long day, that first day in Berlin. Surveying the physical devastation was emotionally exhausting. Contemplating the condition of the population was paralysing.

A man standing on the road opposite the Reichstag stared fixedly at me for a minute or two while I took photographs, swooped wildly on a cigarette butt I threw down and then set off running as if hell's gates were opening at his heels.

A ragged character sidled up beside me when I was looking up at the Reichschancellery eagles. 'Good day, sir,' he said. 'You are English, no? This must be very interesting for you. It is for me, too. I have just come to Berlin. I am Jewish, you see... My father, my wife and my four children were taken to Dachau in 1943, but I...well, I am a very good electrician.' He grinned again.

A couple — a thin, long-faced man and a woman in a moulting fur coat clinging to his arm as if never to let him go — accosted me in the Tiergarten. 'Excuse me, sir, but I wonder if you could spare a cigarette? I am not German. I am Dutch. My wife and I have been working at Saxenhausen. We are walking home...'

'Yes, sir, I am Dutch also. For me? The packet? Oh, you are too generous. My husband cannot smoke much. It is a great comfort when one is hungry, but it makes him cough. He has trouble with his lungs and sleeping out in this weather is very bad for him.'

An old man in one of the bucket chains hawked and spat and muttered as I walked past. Fear shadowed the eyes of the woman beside him. 'Ssh! Be silent, you blockhead! He will arrest us. Do you want that?'

When I got back to my quarters late in the afternoon a girl of about eighteen years was standing at the main entrance of the building — a plumpish, tidily dressed, respectable-looking girl. An hour later she was still standing there. I asked her what she wanted. She said that she was looking for her aunt, Frau Heinrich Harz.

'This house was been requisitioned,' I said. 'Only the caretakers are here now. They live in the basement. You should enquire there.'

'I have.'

'Well?'

'They say my aunt left here six weeks ago and did not come back.'

'Then what on earth are you waiting for?'

'There is nothing else to do. I think my aunt is dead, perhaps. You see I only had her to go to. I have been living with some people at Spandau, but they went away and never came back, so I thought I would come here to my aunt.'

She did not sound eccentric. She spoke in a quiet, pleasantly pitched voice, as if this were the most normal conversation in the world. Her tale was that her parents had disappeared during the siege of the city. She went to live with casual acquaintances at Spandau. The casual acquaintances disappeared. She lived on in their house until the food in the cellar was exhausted and then came to look for her aunt.

'Have you no friends in Berlin?' I asked.

'No, none. None at all. We used to live in the country until mother came to work in the shell factory.'

'Is there no one to whom you can go?'

'No one at all. I don't know what I shall do. Can I sleep here?'

'No, it is forbidden. Have you got any money?'

'No.'

'Well, I'm sorry I can't help you. You must go to some

German family about here and ask where you can sleep. Have you any food?'

She spread her hands. She wore brown cloth gloves.

'I am sorry I can't help you,' I repeated.

'Thank you,' she said politely. 'It will be all right.'

She walked off down the dark street weeping quietly.

Two days later the Russians hung an enormous portrait of Stalin on the Brandenburger Tor and Red Army girls were directing the traffic on the Unter den Linden with flagged batons and robotic precision.

A voice beside me: 'Excuse me, sir, is that Stalin? It is? Ah, handsome, handsome is he not? Have you any spare cigarette butts, sir?'

Chapter 13

At the end of my first day in Berlin I was convinced that the city was in its death throes. Human beings could not continue to live in this horrendous garbage heap.

But by the end of my first week I was beginning to change my mind. The bucket chains, the wandering scavengers of cigarette butts, the homeless and the hopeless, crowded the canvas but they were not the whole picture. A community of sorts was gathering itself together in the wreckage. Berliners were getting enough food and water to keep them standing up and, in some residential areas, electric power was available for short periods each day. The wraith of a public transport system had been conjured up to service ration depots and medical aid posts.

Significantly, a black market had sprung up almost as soon as the guns fell silent. Citizens who had managed to save money or small valuables from the devastation could supplement their starvation diet with food from the stocks of secret hoarders or foragers daring enough to raid unrecorded, and therefore unguarded, dumps of military provisions on the outskirts of the city. More and more people were finding employment in public works supervised by the Russians. Here and there, in blocks which had escaped total destruction, shops were opening to sell shoddy, fire-damaged blankets, clothing, footwear and patent medicines. Or acorn coffee, or gut schnapps and watered wine.

Thanks to Russian experience in dealing with the problems of their own devastated cities, epidemic diseases were controlled. The worst was debilitating diarrhoea attributed to a water supply polluted by corpses and sewage. Typhoid, typhus and influenza were to flare later with a flood of refugees from the eastern provinces.

After streets were cleared for the passage of motor traffic, absolute priority went to the repair of water and sewerage works and to the procurement of food from farmlands within a fifty-mile radius — the area from which supplies of perishables were normally drawn.

All in all, I believe that the Soviets in those early days did more to keep Berlin alive than the Anglo-Americans could possibly have done. I base that opinion on the performance of military government in the Ruhr and the Rhineland where lack of planning — indeed lack of any comprehension of what military government would entail in such circumstances — created chaos. The Russian method of maintaining order and achieving results in the essentials was not inhibited by humanitarian niceties. They understood mass psychology. They realised that the sooner Berliners could be encouraged to help themselves, the better it would be for all concerned. The sooner these stunned and aimless millions could be given some hope for a future, some interest beyond the immediate satisfaction of hunger or the avoidance of physical pain, the fewer demands they would make on the resources of the Red Army.

Wherever shreds of community interests or institutions survived, the Russians nurtured them. Within a few weeks of the surrender they encouraged the publication of newspapers. They restored the broadcasting service, permitted the organisation of public entertainments, and announced that they would approve the formation of trade unions and democratic political parties.

The response was at first faint, but it grew stronger rapidly. By the time the British and Americans occupied their allotted zones occasional orchestral concerts were being given in the Opera House, which had escaped severe damage.

Four small daily newspapers were on sale. Three political 'parties' surfaced: the Communists, of course, led by old members who had spent the war underground or had survived the concentration camps; Social Democrats; and a loose alliance of Christian Socialists, Socialists, and United Socialists.

Radio, newspapers, politics, concerts... The Russians had cleverly nurtured regrowth in a desert of misery. They had shown a measure of mercy to the followers of the beast dead in its lair under a mountain of shattered stone. But Berliners didn't see things that way.

Everywhere there was the same whispered story: 'Thank God you British and Americans have come... We cannot tell how glad we are to see you... Russians are animals — ravening animals. The Russians have taken everything I possess, even my change of clothes. They rape and steal and shoot...'

Anti-Russian hysteria was so strident, so many tales of Russian atrocities circulated, that the chief of the Anglo American public relations bureau saw fit to summon correspondents to issue a 'guidance'.

'Remember,' he said, 'that there is a strong and concerted movement among the German people to sow seeds of distrust and discord between the Allies. Germans believe that they can gain much by dividing us. I wish to warn you against believing German stories about Russian atrocities without thoroughly checking them.'

The idea that the German people in their present condition could be strong and concerted about anything struck me as more than a little naive. Anyway, Russophobia was nothing new. The troops had encountered it all the way from the Rhine as they met thousands of panic-stricken civilians fleeing westward.

The Russians were coming! Anything on God's earth to escape the Russians! Any heel was better than a Russian heel!

When you singled out individuals from the stampeding mass and questioned them, it almost always turned out they had no first-hand knowledge of Russians at all. They had been told this. They had heard that — from a friend or a brother or a cousin who had served on the Eastern Front...

Certainly Hitler had lied to them. His master-race theories were absurd, his claim that the British were decadent and all Jews subhuman the raving of a disordered mind — but about the Bolsheviks, the Führer had been right!

Goebbels's propaganda had scored at least one success which would survive the disillusion of defeat. It had instilled into the German people a psychotic fear of the 'hordes from the East'. When the Red Army advanced to the outskirts of Berlin a wave of suicide swept the city.

Dr Ferdinand Friedensburg — who as director of the Institute of Economic Research and chief of Berlin Police in the days of the Weimar Republic could be presumed to have a proper respect for figures — estimated that between 30 000 and 40 000 Berliners took their own lives in May and June. Suicide was a way out, an escape from the unbearable tensions created by day and night bombing and shelling, overwork, and fear that the future promised nothing but humiliation and suffering in alien bondage.

How much had Russian behaviour, as distinct from an unreasoning fear of Bolsheviks, fuelled this orgy of self-destruction?

I put the question to scores of Berliners of both sexes. Discounted for exaggerations, the picture that emerged was credible. The Red Army overran the city in the white heat of battle, fired by a thirst for vengeance. They destroyed, looted and raped in much the same way as the German Army — by the accounts of Polish refugees — had destroyed, looted and raped Poland and Western Russia four years previously.

The most objective account of Russian behaviour came from a middle-aged woman, wife of an oil technician. I took notes of the interview.

Q: *You say the Russians behaved very brutally after the fighting. What do you mean by 'brutally'?*
A: They looted houses, shot anyone who resisted them, and attacked women. They lost all control.

Q: *What happened when they looted a house? Can you tell me about a house you saw looted? Did they loot your house?*

A: Yes, all these flats were looted. After the firing stopped up the street, ten or eleven soldiers came up the stairs and started kicking and beating on the doors. We were afraid to open, so they broke the locks or kicked them down.

Q: *Then what happened?*

A: They looked everywhere to see if there were any arms or snipers. Then some of them started pulling open drawers and throwing things about, and others attacked the women.

Q: *What do you mean by attacked? Did they rape the women?*

A: Mostly, yes.

Q: *All of them? Did all the Russian soldiers rape, or try to rape the women?*

A: Not all — most of them. They were drunk. They had bottles of brandy and wine and they were excited — you understand how it would be.

Q: *How many women were in this building?*

A: There were eight of us, I think. Three were in my flat with me.

Q: *Were you raped?*

A: No. One of them came at me, but I speak a little Russian and I told him he was drunk and a disgrace to his country. I told him to tell the others to leave the women alone.

Q: *Did that stop him?*

A: Yes. He was only a boy. He seemed ashamed, but he took all my clothes out of the drawers and wardrobes. He said the Germans had taken all the Russian women's clothes in 1941, so he didn't see why he shouldn't have what he wanted. I didn't try to stop him.

Q: *Didn't he try to stop the others?*

A: They were all drunk. The Russians are terrible when they are drunk. You have no idea what they are like.

Q: *How do you know the other women were raped?*

A: I saw a Russian rape my friend.

Q: *Violently?*

A: Yes.

Q: *But you did not actually see what happened to the others?*

A: No, but there was no doubt about it. They weren't lying It really happened, I assure you.

Q: *Wasn't this just an isolated instance?*

A: No. It happened all over the district. They went to every house in the street.

Q: *What, the same gang?*

A: No, other gangs. It happened all over Berlin. I am not exaggerating. It really happened. At least half the young women in Berlin have been raped by Russians. The trouble went on for days after the fighting stopped.

Q: *Did the Russian officers not try to control their troops?*

A: Of course. Most of the officers were very nice. If you could only get to an officer you were usually all right. We heard that some of the soldiers had been caught in the act and shot. But it was no good complaining. If the officers didn't see it, they wouldn't believe.

Q: *When did this sort of behaviour stop?*

A: It never did stop entirely. The trouble was the wine and brandy stocks. They should have been destroyed. The troops would get drunk at night and the trouble would start up all over again. They were only really bad when they were drunk. They were different when you got to know them. We were lucky in this district — we had one lot for ten days billeted in this house. We were sorry to see them go, because we were afraid of what would happen when a new lot came in.

They were childish, really. Sometimes after trouble they would come in the morning and apologise and ask you not to tell. They would give you some food, just to be friendly and make amends.

Q: You said people were shot. Did you actually see any cases of civilians being shot?

A: A woman I knew up the street was killed.

Q: Did you see her body?

A: Yes. Her sister and I buried her in the garden.

Q: Why was she shot?

A: The Russians thought she had a revolver.

Q: Had she a revolver?

A: No. She had no revolver.

Baffling people, these Russians! Rape and apology. Theft atoned by gifts of food. The savage sacking of a blasted city and, within days, attempts to rehabilitate it...

There were other anomalies. Stories about Kurfurstendamm nightclubs being open again turned out to be true. Eventually I made a round of these cabarets, starting with the notorious Femina near the Potsdammerplatz and the Kaiser Wilhelm Memorial Church. The church was so shot up its walls seemed to waver against the sky, but the building that housed the cabaret stood like an island in an ocean of fallen bricks, twisted girders and masonry in which floated a macabre scum of rotting mattresses, torn curtains, picture frames and debris that included enamel chamber-pots.

The evening was mild and damp. The sewer and corpse smell was in the air. The facade of the Femina was covered with futuristic nudes and tinsel announcements in four languages.

A man with a square, bald head and a pink roly-poly neck greeted patrons in the lobby. He wore an ersatz dinner suit that had been out in the rain, and his job was to smile, wave patrons obsequiously to the ticket office and restrict the influx of soliciting prostitutes to those known and approved by the management.

The cover charge was only two marks fifty but everything was all-wool, yard-wide nightclub. The concussion cracks in the walls had been plastered up and painted. The lights had amber shades. The upholstery was red plush. The waiters wore tails so long they swept the floor, though the garments themselves were so ancient they had a greenish luminescence.

The dance floor and tables were crowded with Russian, British and American officers escorting (or hunting for) personable female companions. A bottle of bad wine cost twenty-five dollars, a horsemeat hamburger and potatoes ten dollars, a pack of American cigarettes a breathtaking twenty dollars.

Berlin women had been without cosmetics for more than a year. But inside the Femina cheeks were as delicately tinted and lips as tacky-looking as if Hitler had won his war. A number of women wore sheer silk stockings.

A mistress of ceremonies in a sequined dress introduced the floor show in German, Russian, English and French. This provoked a philosophic quip from a captain of Soviet field artillery at the table next to mine. He leaned over and remarked in tolerable English: 'So soon from the national to the international! Are not the bombs of your RAF fine professors of foreign languages, no?'

The first turn was a child-dancer — very thin, very light on her feet, and very, very aged. I remembered a complaint by Dr Edward Tokes, entrepreneur of a German variety show organised and licensed a few weeks before to entertain American troops in Weimar. Tokes had bewailed the fact he would never be able to improve the quality of revue while the ballet refused to practise on a diet of 1100 calories a day.

The child-dancer was, however, followed by a contortionist in fair condition, a guitarist, and a contralto whose repertoire ranged from *C'etait une Histoire d'Armour*, through *St Louis Blues* to *Lili Marlene*. After that a troupe of 'Russian' dancers came on. They were so energetic and so popular with the Red Army men that I felt sure they drew supplementary rations as heavy industrial workers. Then there was a boogie-woogie band which only a New Yorker could have distinguished from the genuine article.

I had always heard Hitler discouraged this sort of degenerate debauchery among the pure of blood, so I asked the band leader how he managed to keep so well up-to-date with his paperwork in spite of the wicked Nazis.

He confided that he employed two Hungarian fiddlers whom he sent home on vacation every six months. On the way back they always managed to stow a few American dance records in their suitcases. The records reached Budapest by way of Buenos Aires and Berne. Part scores were then transcribed. If any overzealous Gestapo man became too curious, the handwritten sheet music could be produced to prove that the number was really a pure Aryan composition. Sometimes when the hunting of the Hungarian fiddlers was lean, the clarinettist — who had a freak musical memory — risked it in the interests of his art and listened to BBC dance sessions.

Russian officers made up a fair percentage of the Femina's male clientele, but a surprising number of able-bodied Germans went there, too. Some of them were industrial technicians, specialists upon whom the Soviet authorities smiled benignly. But who the rest were I did not try very diligently to find out. Pimps, black marketeers, spies... There were probably more ears trained to catch whispered asides in the Femina than in any other establishment of the sort east of Lisbon or north of the Bosphorus. Ears well-enough trained could command generous hire even in the country of a vanquished enemy. One must always beware of one's friends.

The Femina was not Berlin's only 'luxury' entertainment. A commissionaire in a magnificent orange uniform turned away a surplus of would-be customers from the plate-glass doors of the Cafe Leon and Kabarett der Kommiker. In the Kommiker the star turn was a cadaverous comedian miming a Berliner eating an invisible dinner. Here also one heard a new song hit, *Berlin Will Rise Again*. The bucket chains were already humming it.

Besides these Kurfurstendamm cabarets a number of smaller cafes and restaurants with floor shows opened up. In them one could sit sipping unsweetened ersatz coffee, chemical orangeade and off-colour claret, watching and listening. In all of them the price of a whore was, on the average, five cigarettes. In all of them the already vast black market in food, tobacco and loot was flourishing. One could obtain a passable Dresden figurine for a tin of cheese and bacon out of a K ration carton; or a camera for half-a-dozen bars of chocolate; or even the tenancy of a slightly cracked apartment for ten litres of petrol originally hoarded against the need to flee the horrors of *Bolshevismus*.

In the early days of the tripartite occupation of Berlin, correct, if by no means cordial, relations existed between the elements of military government. If one was to believe the official handouts, everybody loved everybody else and all parties were cooperating wholeheartedly in the task of keeping the four million inhabitants of the city fed and putting them to work on reconstruction.

But the truth was otherwise and that soon became evident. The Russians had no intention of cooperating with anybody. They appeared to suffer from a malignant inferiority complex which made them increasingly touchy and aggressive when trivial differences of opinion arose over procedures and the allocation of responsibilities. They cheated blatantly in matters of larger concern. Serious friction occurred when they denied their Western partners permission to procure an equitable share of farm produce from the rural belt around the city. This land, they announced, was within the Eastern occupation zone allotted to them at Yalta and any food it produced would be distributed only to the population in the parts of the metropolis under Russian control. Since the British and Americans insisted on their right to share in the occupation of the capital, they could make their own arrangements to feed their own dependents from resources farther afield.

From the beginning it was apparent that Soviet policy aimed to force the Western Powers out of Berlin and concede another propaganda victory.

Mutterings about 'kicking the shit out of the Commies' subsided but, there was no fraternisation between off-duty Tommies, GIs and Ivans. Although a certain brittle camaraderie existed between officers patronising the nightclubs, among other ranks the atmosphere was strained. The Soviet garrison troops were sullenly unfriendly. A high proportion of them were illiterate Asiatics, and the Tommies and GIs decided they were only a bunch of unwashed savages who used bathtubs for latrines.

Dislike of Russians was by no means confined to Berlin where contact with them was closest. Their unwillingness to consult or cooperate in formulating a common policy for dealing with the defeated Germans alarmed even the most optimistic of political observers in the Anglo-American zones. Moscow pre-empted interference with its pre-determined objectives by piling one fait accompli on another without pause.

The mass eviction of German farmers from Sudetenland was a case in point. It began as soon as the Red Army had won control of the territory annexed by Hitler in 1938. On the road to Pilsen in June, I met long columns of refugees streaming back towards the Danube — not liberated slave workers but displaced smallholders ordered off their allotments without warning.

The summer had been fiercely hot and dry, and yellow dust rose in clouds from the sideroads where the columns of handcarts and waggons drawn by ox or horse crawled along, head to tail. The refugees were sunburnt leathery-brown. They were clad in rags stained by weather and travel. The pinch of hunger was already upon them. The children lay almost naked in the canvas-covered carts, their faces streaked with grime and tears. The older people plodded behind, or came forward to throw their weight on the wheels when the skinny draught animals baulked on the hills. The eyes of the evicted were hard with misery.

The first time I encountered one of these columns, a bullock cart had lost a wheel and lay swivelled across the road. While the jeep driver yelled 'Gangway', I leaned out and shouted at an old man: 'Who are you people? Are you Germans?'

'Yes.'

'Where are you going?'

'God knows.'

'How many of you are there?'

'God knows that, too.'

'Why are you travelling?'

'The Russians ordered us out of our homes.'

A dozen women, barefoot and half-naked, pushed the crippled cart into the ditch. My driver accelerated, smothering the wretched procession in exhaust smoke and dust.

The rain of Russian retribution was falling on the just and unjust alike. I learned later that many of these people were not jumped-up settlers occupying appropriated *Lebensraum* in Bohemia but German nationals expelled from land they had owned legally and worked productively for generations.

These precipitate, unselective expulsions were costly. In Prague President Beneš himself protested. Could Czecho-slovakia, he asked, restore its agriculture and industry survive the postwar crisis, without help from three million pairs of hardworking hands?

The Sudeten expulsions were not the worst. In August and September the Berlin railway stations began to receive trainloads of diseased, famine-stricken refugees from Silesia and East Prussia. They died in hundreds, lying on platforms awash with filth. I walked through sidings where trucks were piled with corpses, and where women stewed dog-meat and turnips in blackened cans beside heaps of human dung.

One of them plucked at my jacket sleeve, pointed to her mouth and hissed: '*Essen, essen!*' I wondered if she, simply because she was German, deserved less pity than the living skeletons down the hill at Buchenwald.

I realised then that the war had not ended with the execution and dismemberment of Hitler's Germany. There were other beasts in other lairs.

Berlin, 1945
Photograph: Osmar White

Part V

QUESTIONS &
REFLECTIONS

Chapter 14

One day on a lonely road in the Hunsrück, Charlie the Demon Driver and I decided to eat lunch in a clearing by the edge of a pine forest. Charlie ran the jeep up a sidetrack. We got out, climbed a few yards up a slope and sat down in the grass.

It was still, clear spring. In the valley we could see the chimney of a farmhouse peeping over a plantation of shelter trees. In the far distance was the Rhenish plain, chequered with ploughland and pasture. Behind us the trees marched down from the mountains. The air was perfumed with resin and new growth. There were no sounds of war.

For a while we just sat and looked, feeling the pleasant weight of sun on our shoulders. Charlie unwrapped his K ration and started eating. I said: 'It's a beautiful country, Charlie. It must have been good to live in before the war.'

'I guess so,' Charlie said.

Charlie was a morose young man. He didn't talk very much, but when he did, he always managed to let you know he thought the world a pretty sour place — except, maybe, for the small New Hampshire town he came from. The army, any army, was full of Charlies — men who only wanted to go home.

After we had been sitting a while, I saw someone coming up the road from the direction of the farm. He was a boy about nine or ten years old, barefooted, in short grey pants and jersey, carrying a stick. Twenty or thirty yards away from the jeep he stopped, looked doubtfully at us and it, and stood switching the stick in the grass.

Charlie munched his crackers stolidly, looking at the child. Then he said: 'Yeh, I guess so. A pretty beautiful country. Pity the suckers couldn't stay in it and make the most of it. There looks plenty of living room to me.'

'Guess you're right, Charlie.'

'Yeh,' he said. 'I'm right. I hate the sonsofbitches. All the krauts.'

'Well, the world's got reason to,' I said.

'Yeh,' he said.

There was silence again. The boy stopped switching his stick. Curiosity had overcome his fear. We didn't look savage. We had no gun in sight. He walked round the jeep inspecting it, then came nearer.

He was a sturdy child, with a shock of brown hair, a snub nose, and wide-open blue eyes. He was evidently consumed with curiosity. He studied the K ration wrappings with intense interest, then us. He smiled, faintly.

'Get the hell out of it, you dirty little shit,' Charlie said in a low tone, '*go on, scram!*'

The boy's face split into a grin.

'He's all right, Charlie,' I said, 'let him be. I want to talk to him afterwards.'

Charlie grunted.

'Listen, Charlie,' I went on, 'pretty soon this war's going to be over. We're going to win — and we've got to do something with the krauts. Have you ever thought about that?'

'I know what ought to be done with them. They ought to be wiped out.'

'Has a kraut ever done anything to you?'

He looked at me suspiciously. 'What do you mean?'

'I mean have you got anything against the krauts — personally?'

He smiled. 'I'm over here, aren't I?'

'Yes. But what I'm getting at is: what do you, yourself, have against Germans?'

'They kicked people about, didn't they? They couldn't stay in their own goddamn country. They murdered Jews and tortured people. They wanted to be the big shots in the world. That's right, isn't it? Well, they ought to be wiped out.'

'Look at that kid, Charlie,' I said. 'What's he done to you or anybody else? What are you going to do about him?'

Charlie stared.

'What's your name, boy?' I asked.

'Erich.'

'Do you live on the farm down there?'

'Yes, sir.'

'Is your father at home?'

'Yes, sir.'

'What is his work? Is he a farmer?'

'No, sir. He is a woodcutter.'

He looked like a nice child. He had a gentle voice and there was something appealing in the way he faced us, in the way his curiosity had overcome his nervousness. His legs, I saw, were a little misshapen, as if by rickets in infancy.

'Do you like playing soldiers?'

He looked at me doubtfully for a moment and then said: 'Yes, sir.'

'Do you like real soldiers?'

'Yes, sir.'

'Do you love the Führer?'

'No, sir.'

'Who told you to answer that?'

'My father, sir.'

'Listen, Charlie,' I said. 'The kid's father is a woodcutter. He lives on the farm down there. He says he likes playing soldiers, but he doesn't love the Führer because his father told him not to. What the hell! Are you going to wipe that kid out, too?'

Charlie looked at him, darkly and bitterly. 'Look at him,' he said. 'Fat. Healthy. Fresh. Did you ever see a Belgian kid that was fat and healthy and fresh? This little bastard is no good. He hasn't got a chance. Twenty-five years from now he'll be just another storm-trooper for another Hitler. Yes, sure I'd wipe him out. Why the hell not? He hasn't got a chance. Twenty-five years from now he'll be trying to poke a bayonet through my kid's guts.'

'Then you mean it. You're for wiping this kid out?'

'Yeh.'

'Why don't you? There's nothing to stop you. You could wipe plenty of kraut civilians out, couldn't you, these days?'

Charlie spat disgustedly. 'Okay,' he said. 'Okay. I get it. I haven't got the nerve. None of us have got the nerve. So what? Another twenty-five years and this kid tries to poke a bayonet through my kid's guts. *So he ought to be wiped out. That's the sensible way.*'

We let it lie. I asked the child a few more questions. He gained confidence and sat down on the grass a short distance away. I wondered if, in his secret mind, he was dreaming childish dreams of heroism — of killing us, the hated invaders of the fatherland, with a machine-pistol and of being decorated by the Führer before the Party rally at Nuremberg. He didn't look as if he were dreaming. There was only curiosity in his eyes — curiosity about life.

Suppose it were proven that the extermination of all Germans was the best thing for humanity, would I have the nerve to kill that child? If I knew that he would one day try to kill a child of mine — would I have the nerve to kill him to prevent it?

Silly question...

When we got up to go, Charlie was still glowering, but he thrust the chocolate bar and stick of gum from his K ration into the child's hands.

'Here, you dirty little sonofabitch,' he growled, 'take it.'

So might any man have done, even if he had pulled the trigger of a thousand bomb releases and killed a thousand little boys like Erich.

In many ways Charlie the Demon Driver was archetypal of the British and American soldiers who fought their way across Germany to the Elbe. They believed implicitly that they were fighting in a just cause: to destroy an intolerably depraved and vicious enemy. They were angry men, enraged men when they learned the truth about the concentration camps. But when the shooting stopped their rage did not last for long.

The proclaimed policy of Allied Military Government was to restore and preserve order in occupied Germany, to find and punish those guilty of war crimes and crimes against humanity, and to revive the moral perception of the German people by bringing home to them full realisation of their guilt in supporting Hitler. Ostracism would make the point.

The no-fraternisation rule, promulgated as soon as German territory was occupied, never worked. It was absurdly artificial and unenforceable. Primarily it was aimed at discouraging the cohabitation of British and American soldiers with German women. But as soon as the fighting was over and troops could settle into semipermanent billets, a considerable number of officers and other ranks, particularly Military Government personnel, established liaisons with German women; liaisons in every category from common prostitution to genuine and often star-crossed love affairs.

To my own knowledge, soldiers who served in the American division which liberated Buchenwald in April were sleeping with German girls by the end of May. They boasted about it.

When the camp itself was cleaned up and converted into a centre for DPs, the row of huts in which hundreds of Eastern Europeans had died of disease and starvation was refurnished with looted furniture from Weimar, and used as a brothel.

It flourished and supplied the camp with uncounted cases of canned food and cartons of cigarettes bought at the American PX in the town.

My notebooks of the time are full of the transcripts of interviews with soldiers about non-fraternisation.

I asked a PFC from Minnesota:

Q: *Then you don't believe that all Germans are guilty*
     for supporting Hitler, and they ought to be punished?
A: Hell, it's no use talking like that. Do you think
     I'm guilty for Roosevelt getting elected President?
     I'm a Republican. What could I do about Roosevelt
     getting elected President? It was the same with a lot
     of Germans.Germans are folks just like you and me.
     My grandpop was German. Was he guilty for Hitler?
     I don't think this girl I'm screwing was guilty for
     Hitler, any more than I'm guilty for Roosevelt.
     If the President blows it then we all suffer, see?
     It's not who's guilty and who isn't. We all
     suffer — the ones who voted for him and the
     ones who didn't...

A technical sergeant's comment: 'Saying all Germans are bad just because they're Germans is what Hitler said about Jews, isn't it? This kraut family is all right. Decent folks, like lots I know at home. I'm good and mad at Hitler and the SS boys. I know all that stuff about the camps but now they're beaten, so what?'

And this statement from a tank crewman: 'These kraut dames are all right, see? They know what it's for. I'd be a sucker to fall for all this no-frat shit. What about the broads the MG officers have hired for secretaries? Did you ever see a homely German dame working in MG?

Cigarettes, chocolate, candy, K rations, were now known as 'frat bait'. No-fraternisation was a joke like Prohibition.

In the end officialdom bowed to the inevitable with hilarious solemnity. Shortly after the surrender, SHAEF announced that the no-fraternisation order had been relaxed to permit Allied soldiers to converse with and make small gifts to German children. Such was the wisdom of the 'experts' charged with the responsibility of revising the moral perception of the German people.

Soon after the occupation of Berlin a further relaxation of the rule for British troops was announced, but the order was countermanded when a popular columnist in a Sunday newspaper claimed that it would have a disastrous effect on the morale and morals of the women of Great Britain.

The sanest comment I heard on the fiasco came from a Munich physician, a genuine anti-Nazi: 'If your leaders really wish to convince Germans that the Nazis were wrong as well as unsuccessful, they should avoid the mistakes made by our military government in occupied territories. Brutally severe penalties inflicted on whole communities for acts of rebellion by a few individuals nourished the French resistance at a time when Germany was as much the master of Europe as the Allies are today; and they compounded the error by subjecting the population to unnecessary humiliations. If you want to insure against a rebirth of Fascism, you must demonstrate that discipline can be imposed without terrorism, or for that matter without pettifogging restriction on normal human relationships.'

A Berlin washerwoman expressed an opinion: 'Hitler's girls will soon take your soldiers to bed and make them forget their orders. They don't think there's anything wrong in doing it. They'll have their fun and laugh and joke afterwards. F---ing doesn't mean anything any more. You'll see — before long they'll be letting Negroes and Jews f---k them.'

There was probably some truth in it. Hitler's immaculate Aryan maidens may have subscribed to the master-race teachings of the Nazi idealogues but their puritanical inhibitions did not long survive sexual deprivation.

After a few sordid and pointless courts martial of scapegoats, the no-fraternisation rule was eased quietly into limbo. The policy of sending the female Hun to Coventry for the good of her political soul fizzled out ignominiously.

The announced policy of de-Nazifying Germany by removing from positions of authority all members and active supporters of the National Socialist Party was almost as silly as the no-fraternisation edict. When the German armies were defeated the civil administration of the country collapsed totally. It has been run, very largely if not wholly, by loyal

Party members or their sycophants. These people bolted, or tried to bolt, as the invaders approached. Essential services ceased to operate until Allied Military Government took over and rounded up any municipal officials, policeman, technicians and tradesmen they could find and put them to work in their old jobs. Sorting the sheep from the goats could wait until water taps ran again, sewers worked and gas and electricity supplies were restored to habitable buildings.

The harassed, overworked officials attempting to restore order in communities fragmented by defeat gave little thought to identification of war criminals. Political intelligence units traced and arrested many big-shot Nazis: politicians and bureaucrats and the most notorious executioners and torturers in the death camps. They ignored small fry whose crimes were adjudged less heinous only because they involved fewer victims.

Industrial executives and the top men in banking and financial institutions seemed exempt from arrest. Scientific researchers and highly qualified technicians in the armaments industries were rarely investigated. They enjoyed the status of highly coveted booty, particularly if they were jet-propulsion or rocketry experts.

I visited the Zeiss optical laboratories and factories in Jena before the town was officially occupied. Senior members of the research staff calmly, smugly, informed me that they had already been promised well-paid jobs in the United States and were awaiting evacuation. Their only anxiety was that the Russian tanks would get to town first and they would be forced to accept less well-paid employment behind the Urals.

Later I learned that cloak-and-dagger teams of American and Russian agents were energetically competing with one another to locate and kidnap top German scientists and smuggle them out of the country. Clashes were frequent and both sides incurred casualties.

The Russians were already plundering the country of more than Nazi brains. They were dismantling the most sophisticated equipment of heavy industry in the eastern zone and shipping it away by the trainload together with teams of engineers.

In practice, then, de-Nazifying Germany meant skimming the most offensive scum off the melting pot into which the parts of the dismembered nation had been thrown, destroying it with judicial pomp and ceremony, and reducing what was left to a broth from which reparations could be distilled.

Adult Germans had been de-Nazified by the abject defeat of Hitler's regime. Chastising them with payback could teach them nothing they did not already know. But what about the future for little boys like Erich whose father had warned him not to say he loved the Führer? Would he turn out to be a carrier of the *Herrenvolk* virus?

Chapter 15

For three months or more after the Rheims surrender, the most important and difficult task faced by the occupying Powers was to assure the physical survival of the German civilian population by procuring and distributing enough food to stave off outright famine, and by creating some sort of social structure within which order could be preserved and self-help encouraged.

The end of the war in the Far East in August/September 1945 marked, I believe, the point at which the sense of crisis in Germany began to diminish.

The spectre of approaching European winter was less terrifying now that killing enemies on the other side of the world no longer had first call on the resources of the Allies. There was less talk about 'kicking the shit out of the Commies', although the hard-core pessimists still muttered that Uncle Sam would have to do it with an atom bomb sooner or later.

At the grassroots, military government was working. The population remained completely docile, even after the first shock of defeat had worn off. This baffled me. How could people whose morale and will to fight on had withstood the savage punishment inflicted by the saturation bombings of their cities in 1944 and 1945 now be so ready to bow obsequiously to foreign authority and protest that they had never subscribed to Nazi doctrine or condoned Nazi brutality.

Perhaps the key to the riddle was a propensity built into the German character, an instinct to obey orders issued by those in power, without question or protest. In Hitler's Reich discipline had become a drug of dependency — the opium of the people.

Once, on the way to interview British war prisoners released from a camp near Cassel, I stopped in a village square to get hot water for coffee. There was a great flurry to oblige at the inn and at last a neatly dressed cadaverous little man came out with a pitcher of hot water and two cups on a napkin-covered tray. He spoke fluent English and was anxious to show it off. It turned out he was an accountant who had spent some years in the London office of a woollen goods firm. Like 99 per cent of civilians he fawned. He was overjoyed — absolutely overjoyed — to see an Englishman again. He has so many good friends in England, so many excellent friends! Ach, indeed, the happiest years of his life had been the years in London.

By this time I was getting a little tired of Germans with warm, friendly feelings for the English and I was irritated by his description of the no-fraternisation rule as 'so unfortunate, so unfortunate!'

'Look,' I said, coming to the point more rapidly than usual, 'there has been a war on, you know. Has it ever occurred to you that perhaps your English friends wouldn't be quite so glad to see you?'

His face fell. He registered sadness and Christian forgiveness. He went through the now nauseatingly familiar routine of explaining how the Nazis weren't the German people, how the German people were the unhappy victims of thugs and gangsters.

'In that case,' I said, 'the German nation must have produced proportionately more thugs and gangsters than any other nation in history. You know damned well that there were millions of Nazis — and you can take it from me that I don't think any the better of them because there's no one outside the POW cages who will admit it.'

The little accountant's face fell even lower and when he spoke again I am inclined to think he spoke sincerely for the first time.

'I know,' he said, 'I know. But I tell you the truth when I say I don't understand where all the Nazis came from... Just members of the Party, yes. One can understand that — but not the SS. My God, the SS!'

Soon afterwards he took back the empty pitcher and the cups without conversation having produced anything very profitable on either side. But he had set me thinking. One of the few things seemingly genuine in this 'innocent victim patter' was a repeatedly expressed fear and detestation of the SS. As time went on I collected more evidence that it was not assumed. Even in the fighting forces the Party strongmen were a breed apart.

When the remnants of the German armies in Italy came through the Brenner Pass to surrender to the forces of Patton and Patch in Bavaria, I went down to see the show and do interviews in the great prisoner-of-war compounds on Tegernsee.

The Germans were coming into the assembly areas by corps and divisions, still fully armed, and still in formation. It was a strange sensation to drive for miles past columns of infantry, artillery, SS troops, specialist units, all marching in perfect order and shepherded by swastika-decked, bemedalled officers in shiny staff cars; and still stranger to see traffic directed by German military policemen with light machine-guns set up at their control posts.

The lake district had become an enormous open-air prison compound fenced only by the mountains, and guarded only by a few tanks, flak waggons and armoured cars. Patch's and Patton's men gave up trying to organise the surrender in any detail. They simply told the German commanders where to go and gave them authority to obtain and distribute food and medical supplies from captured army depots.

The amazing Nazi military machine continued to function. Discipline was preserved even under the most difficult conditions. The men at first slept in the fields without shelter. For several weeks they very nearly starved.

Soon rows of neat, shoulder-high shelters sprang up, built from poles cut in the forest, lumber from sawmills, odds and ends of roofing and shingles from farms, stones, turf and hay. These camps were laid out in blocks and streets. Cookhouses, 'hospitals', latrines and bathing places were provided. The men were required to shave and do what they could to keep their now ragged uniforms clean and presentable. Military policemen patrolled to see that rules were rigidly observed. American officers with the guard units were very impressed.

'You've got to hand it to these krauts,' one company commander said. 'I don't suppose there's another army in the world like the German army for organisation and discipline — even after it's had its pants beaten off! No wonder these bastards could fight the rest of the world — and so damned near beat it!'

A naive discovery of the virtues which had given German national vice such enormous stature, perhaps... But there are some truisms which do not lose force by demonstration.

'They obey their own orders, all right — but do they obey yours?' I asked.

'To the letter,' he replied. 'There's only one thing...you can't mix SS and Wehrmacht. They hate one another's guts! Why, a Wehrmacht man hates an SS man a damned sight more than he hates you or me!'

That, I thought, would bear further inquiry. Compounds for Wehrmacht and SS men were usually divided by a road, sometimes by a field. There was a subtle physical difference between the two classes of prisoners. The SS men were bigger, better nourished and more uniform in type. They did not, however, look markedly brutal or brainless. They looked tough, though no more tough than Americans, British or French might have looked, living under similar circumstances. The difference between them and the scraggier Wehrmacht was about as marked as that between a territorial and a regular regiment in the British Army.

The American officer's remark that the two groups hated one another was borne out by general behaviour. Seldom did one see a Wehrmacht man and an SS man talking together. Fatigue parties passed one another in stony silence. Officers did not salute, except at formal meetings. There were no shouted conversations across the dividing road between the compounds.

I made more direct inquiry. One of the Wehrmacht officers whom I questioned about camp conditions was a young, intelligent and — as far as I could judge — frank man. He was neither sullen nor effusive. He answered questions concisely and, where he believed further explanation was called for, he insisted courteously but firmly on giving it.

'There is one thing I'd like to ask you about, captain,' I said, 'but I don't want you to feel obliged to answer. What is the cause of the obvious bad feeling between the Wehrmacht and SS troops?'

He looked at me thoughtfully for a moment, then said: 'I don't know how much you know about German politics in the last two years — but there has been a great division of opinion between the Army and the Party. The SS has always been considered to be the executive force behind the Party edicts.'

'Can you explain further?'

'I can speak only for the opinion of Wehrmacht officers. Most of us think that Party interference in strategy had been the main cause of our defeat.'

'The differences of the Party and the Army,' I said, 'have been fairly well understood by the world since the attempt to kill Hitler on 20 July. But how has this hostility communicated itself to all ranks? The July attempt was not a popular revolution. Whatever disagreements existed at high levels they have hardly been reflected in your fighting forces.'

'You think not?' He smiled. 'Did the Wehrmacht really fight as well as the SS?'

'Perhaps not. But we have always regarded the SS as elite regiments — picked men.'

'Yes, they were picked,' he said, almost inaudibly.

'For physique and political reliability?'

'Yes.'

'How was their political reliability judged?'

'Any young man who had been an enthusiastic member of the Hitler Youth was thought politically reliable. The Hitler Youth was a selective organisation,' he said.

'I thought the SS was a purely volunteer corps.'

'Yes, it was originally. But after the Russian Front casualties became heavy, it was necessary to find replacements with men drafted from the Wehrmacht.'

'How were replacements selected?'

'They were the fittest men, and the men who had clean political records.'

'I thought there were no doubtful political records permitted in Germany?'

He grinned. 'Some were more enthusiastic about the Party and the Leader than others,' he said.

One could appreciate the effect of this dividing the sheep from the goats over a long period. Still…

'Are you suggesting,' I asked, 'that nowadays the SS are the Nazis — the enthusiastic Nazis — and all the Wehrmacht are the anti-Nazis?'

'Surely there are very few enthusiastic Nazis any more,' he said dryly. 'It is just that some stayed enthusiastic longer than others.'

'You don't sound like a Nazi yourself. Were you a member of the Party?'

That, I thought, will blow him out. He'll turn out to be just another good, misunderstood, German. But he surprised me.

'Yes,' he replied, 'I was a member of the Party. I was also a member of the Hitler Youth. But I come from an old military family. I don't believe politicians should interfere with the strategy of commanders in the field. I think Germany would have won this war if it had not been for political interference.'

'And you think this is the cause of the bad feeling between the SS and the Wehrmacht?'

'Yes. But only indirectly.'

'What do you mean by "indirectly"?'

'The SS were, as you say, elite troops, so when supplies started to get short they received preferential treatment. In the retreat, Wehrmacht units were sacrificed so SS could get away. SS men fired on Wehrmacht men for disobeying "no retreat" orders. No retreat orders!' His eyes flashed angrily.

'Then it comes down to this: Wehrmacht officers disapproved of political interference with commanders in the field and both officers and men were resentful and jealous of the preference given SS troops. The SS were the police, the watchdogs, to stifle any army revolt?'

'I suppose so. Yes. Of course.'

'What do you think caused the July revolt? Was it an attempt to rid the army of political control because the general staff believed political control was losing the war?'

'There was more to it than that, but what you say is correct, as far as it goes.'

'The attempt failed. Why?'

'It was bungled. It had bad luck. The SS were too strong.'

I asked him about concentration camps. He denied any first-hand knowledge. He said he was not surprised that atrocities had been perpetrated. But, he added politely, he believed Allied propaganda accounts were exaggerated.

I told him angrily I had seen the concentration camps for myself. He could take it from me that the Allied propagandists were by no means exaggerating.

At the change in my voice, he and half-a-dozen other officers who had been listening to the interrogation with great interest, and occasionally discussing a point among themselves in undertones, stiffened to attention. A mask dropped over their faces.

It was always the same... An edge in the voice of someone with the whip hand, and the beaten German — soldier, civilian or political thug — jumped to attention. However intelligent, however convinced of personal rectitude, a German's conditioned reflexes never failed to work...

In the SS headquarters half-a-mile away, the 'supermen' fairly writhed to explain they were really different from the Wehrmacht.

The SS men I had interviewed in POW cages in Luxembourg and Belgium after the Ardennes offensive had often been sullen and arrogant, the world's idea of typical Nazis. But here sullenness and arrogance were difficult to find — as difficult as rudimentary truthfulness. The only helpful man I encountered was an old doctor who produced papers to show that he had been drafted from the medical service of the regular army at the end of 1942. I tackled him promptly about the activities of SS 'scientists'.

'It's no use telling me propaganda is being made about so-called scientific work in concentration camps, Doctor,' I said, 'because I have myself seen specimens of the work, the laboratories in which it was done, the foreign assistants in those laboratories, and their records. What I am trying to find out is *how* the men who did it were recruited.'

'It could not have been important or very important or very useful,' he said, 'or the medical world would have heard of it. I doubt that it could have been done by a greater number of people.'

'It was done by the Waffen SS organisation,' I told him. 'There were plates on laboratory doors indicating it and the records bore the SS device. As an SS medical officer you should have heard of it.'

His weary old eyes met mine. He ran his fingers through a straggly greying beard.

'I did not hear of it,' he said earnestly.

'Nevertheless it was done. Can you suggest by whom and by whose orders?'

'The medical profession is not entirely free from cruelty,' he replied. 'Doctors are just as likely to be insane as men in any other profession — probably more so.' His lips twitched a little.

'Look Doctor,' I said, 'I'm trying to get a picture of the mechanics of this thing. If your commanding officer ordered you to find him a sadist — a torturer who would take pleasure in his work — just how would you go about it?'

He laughed nervously. 'You are joking, perhaps?'

'I am not joking, at all. Suppose, seriously, that you received such an order; and suppose, seriously, you had to obey it, what would you do?'

At last he answered: 'I would look for such a man in prisons,' he said, 'and in military detention barracks.'

'How were men selected from the Waffen SS for concentration-camp duty?' I continued.

'I do not know personally of any men who were selected for it.'

'But you know, presumably, something of the organisation and procedure of the SS. How *would* they be selected?'

'Vacancies would occur and volunteers would be called for. If there were not enough volunteers, men would be drafted. But I tell you I don't actually know of this happening.'

'What sort of men would you expect to volunteer for such work? Good types of men?'

'No,' he spoke a little doubtfully, 'no, not good types. Good types would prefer to stay with their units in the field. Men who perhaps wished to avoid service in the field, or were not content for some reason — or men who thought they would enjoy being gaolers.'

'And if the men had to be drafted?'

'They would choose men who were the least fit physically,' he replied, 'men who were unpopular or inefficient in their units. Detail for such a duty would be considered rather a disgrace for a soldier. There is another thing...' He paused.

'What?' I asked.

'Sometimes men who were convicted of military crimes were sent to concentration camps,' he said. 'They were sent as prisoners. If they behaved themselves they would in time be given certain duties and responsibilities as part of their...rehabilitation.'

How much the old man was trying to underline his point that the rank and file of SS were not thugs and criminals, that they were only 'soldiers obeying orders like any other soldiers', I do not know. But I think that his story was substantially true. It checked.

The process of selecting staff for the concentration camps was diabolically logical. A recipe for dictators in a police state: divide your supporters into the enthusiastic and the not-so-enthusiastic. Sieve the enthusiasts for misfits, perverts and failures who may cause trouble if not controlled. Control them by elevating them to the status of licensed terrorists to intimidate or eliminate the opposition. They will be happy in your service. They will be your most devoted and loyal admirers because you have given them a chance of self-expression.

Chapter 16

Autopsy on the carcass of the Third Reich revealed more subtle indications of the syndrome that destroyed it. Two entries in the record of interviews I compiled after the occupation of the Ruhr cities seem worth quoting at length because the people I questioned impressed me as relatively truthful even if in some respects their opinions differed.

Emil Brunnig. *Volkssturm.* Sheet Metalworker, employed in tank factory of Rheinmetall Borsig complex near Dortmund. Born Bremen, 1894. Married Else Gehard, domestic servant, 1916. Two daughters born 1920, 1926. Service in First World War with infantry regiment on Russian Front, 1916/17. Occupation as metalworker at Krupps which exempted him from earlier call-up. Did not rise from ranks, wounded — shrapnel in chest — March 1917. Health impaired. TB(?).

After 1918 lived on wife's earnings as domestic servant and shop assistant at Dortmund between 1918 and 1920. He then worked odd jobs in foundries and factories through the 1920s with considerable periods of unemployment during which the wife kept the home going. Claims to have been member of Communist Party until 1931, but played little part in local activities. Left Party after election of 1931.

Q: Why did you leave the Communist Party?
A: It was unsafe. I changed my mind anyway. I thought
     the Communists had the wrong idea, that they would

not do the best for Germany. There were too
many Jews in the Party.

Q: *Why don't you like Jews?*

A: Nobody who has lived in Germany would ask
that. The Jews have always been the enemy
of working men. They live on nothing to get
money; then when they have made money
they still live on nothing and go into business
and undersell Germans who can't live on nothing.
The Germans have to give up their businesses.
Jews are hated all over the world — except
in Russia, where they are the government.

Q: *Did you think Hitler was right because he wanted
to stamp out the Jews?*

A: Yes.

Q: *What else do you think was right about Hitler?*

A: I think he wanted to do the best for Germany.

Q: *Do you still think so?*

A: He went wrong when he started the war.

Q: *You know Hitler started the war?*

A: Yes. He marched into Poland.

Q: *Why do you think he started the war?*

A: He had bad advisers. He wanted to make
Germany safe against the Bolshevists.
He thought he could win quickly.

Q: *Then you think Hitler was justified in going to
war to make Germany safe against the Bolshevists?*

A: I don't know. No, I am against war. War is wrong.
It always causes more suffering than it does good.

Q: *Were you better off when Hitler came into power
than you were before?*

A: Yes. I was never out of a job after Hitler came
into power.

Q: *Were wages and conditions good?*

A: Yes, good enough. But it wasn't that. I thought
I would never be out of a job until I got too
old to work.

Q: *Did things get worse after the war started?*
A: Not for two or three years.
Q: *Did you always have enough to eat?*
A: Of course.
Q: *Enough clothes?*
A: Yes. Nobody was very smart, of course, after the war started.
Q: *What were the conditions and hours of work like?*
A: We always had to work long hours. I didn't mind that so much. Everybody had to work long hours. Conditions were not bad until after the air raids started.
Q: *How did conditions become? Bad?*
A: It is obvious. Many workers' houses were hit or burned down. The billeting authority moved five extra families into our block of flats and we were very crowded.
Q: *Were your flats ever hit?*
A: Yes.
Q: *Were any of your family hurt?*
A: Yes. My wife and my daughter Hilda were burned to death in the cellar.
Q: *Where were you?*
A: I was working on the night shift at the factory.
Q: *Where were you when the raid was on?*
A: In the factory shelter. After it was over we went back to work. I did not find out about my wife and daughter until I went home in the morning. War always causes more suffering than it does good.
Q: *Do you hate the English because they killed your wife and daughter?*
A: It was war.
Q: *You knew that German aeroplanes were killing working people in England?*
A: Yes. That is war. War is bad.
Q: *And when was the factory destroyed?*
A: It was destroyed several times — three times.

Q: *Were you out of work for long?*

A: No. I was drafted to another factory.
I am skilled.

Q: *Was everybody drafted to another factory?*

A: Only the skilled workers. Unskilled workers
were put to work on repairs.

Q: *How did the workers feel about the air raids?*
Were they very afraid?

A: At first, yes. We didn't know what was
going to happen. But there was not much
danger in the shelters, the deep shelters.
It was more dangerous at home than at
work. We got good warnings.

Q: *Did you get used to air raids?*

A: Yes we had to.

Q: *Were the workers angry at the English airmen?*

A: Yes, I suppose so. You know how it is.

Q: *Did you ever wish to give up?*

A: No. Nobody wishes to give up.

Q: *Do you think Germany has lost the war?*

A: Yes, Germany is finished.

Q: *When did you first start to think Germany*
was finished?

A: When the Russians started to come back
from Moscow.

Q: *Did nobody wish to give up then? Wouldn't*
it have been better to give up?

A: Yes, it would have been better to give up.
It would have saved much suffering.

Q: *But nobody wanted to give up — why?*

A: I don't understand.

Q: *Why didn't you want to give up when you*
knew Germany couldn't win?

A: There wasn't any way of giving up. Nobody
dared to say Germany was finished. There
were Gestapo in the factory. It would have
been reported.

Q: *Did you ever listen to the British radio?*
A: Sometimes. Everybody did.
Q: *Did you believe what you heard?*
A: It was propaganda. There was more truth in it than in the newspapers. But it was only propaganda.
Q: *Then it didn't make much difference one way or the other?*
A: No. We listened only to find out what was going on.
Q: *But didn't it make you think Hitler was wrong, or give you the idea of giving up?*
A: No. It was only propaganda.
Q: *Then you didn't believe even German propaganda?*
A: No, it was only propaganda.
Q: *Did you ever discuss the news on the British radio with your friends?*
A: Of course not. Someone would have reported it.
Q: *What about your wife and daughters?*
A: My wife was not interested in politics. It was safer not to be interested.
Q: *Did your wife think Hitler was right?*
A: I don't think so, but she was not interested in politics.
Q: *What about your daughters?*
A: They thought Hitler was right.
Q: *Where is your daughter, the one who was not killed?*
A: I don't know. She was married in 1939 and went to live in the east, in Dresden. She never wrote.
Q: *Did your Volkssturm unit fight well when the English came?*
A: We did not fight.
Q: *Why?*
A: It was no use.

Even if he fudged a bit here and there, Emil was a refreshing change from listening to the squirming lies of his fellow prisoners. If you were to believe them, there had never been one dedicated Nazi under Cabinet rank in the whole of Germany:

'Ach, that Hitler! Hitler is a bad man. It had to come to this...'

'Hitler has ruined us, but there are worse men than him — Goebbels and Himmler, they are worse.'

'For long we have seen it coming. We have been ruled by madmen... But what could we do. They shot, beat, tortured anyone who dared to say a word...'

'No, I have never been a member of the Nazi Party...'

'Yes, I told a lie. It is true I had a Party button. I was a postal official. I HAD to be a member of the Party or I would have been out of work. I have a wife and four children and they would have starved. What could I do?'

'No, my children were never really members of the Hitler Youth. I pretended they were delicate, and kept them home...'

'Yes, it is true. Hitler started right, but he came under the influence of wicked men...'

Not long after I spoke to Emil Brunnig an American intelligence officer in Frankfurt suggested I might get a good story out a woman he had interviewed in Bad Nauheim while screening applicants for employment by the Military Government. She was English by birth, married to a Berlin journalist who had arranged for their two small children to be evacuated to the country when the capital came under heavy air attack. Her husband was now missing and the woman was seeking a position as an interpreter.

Frau Constance Schreiner proved willing to talk. A thin, tired-looking blonde in her thirties, she appeared to be highly intelligent, articulate and surprisingly objective in her judgments.

She was the third daughter of an old family of Herefordshire landowners which fell on hard times during the Depression. Before the First World War, a maternal aunt had married a minor German diplomat and Constance often spent summer vacations in Munich. There she met and married her husband, Karl, in 1933.

Schreiner was an intellectual of sorts who believed that Fascism offered a way out for his demoralised nation and he persuaded his wife to this view.

'Until 1937 or 1938,' Frau Schreiner said, 'Hitler's policies worked very well for the great majority of Germans. People had a sense of security and a belief in the future they'd never had before. Even those who had at first opposed the Nazis were converted. Industry prospered from rearmament, there was little unemployment, working conditions improved and, above all, national self-respect was restored. Hitler took over when things were at their worst and, as the Americans say, he delivered the goods he promised.'

'Including persecution of the Jews?' I asked.

She smiled faintly. 'Yes. Anti-Semitism has been deep-rooted in the European middle classes for centuries. It is by no means confined to Germany. Hitler tried to rationalise it with his doctrine of race superiority.'

'But surely,' I said, 'educated Germans didn't swallow that pseudo-scientific hogwash about Aryans being a super-race?'

'Education doesn't come into it,' she answered. 'Educated or not, it's pleasant, reassuring, to be told that you belong to a super-race. The educated English believe it without being told. I know, because I come from that sort of family. The English believe they're so superior they haven't got to worry about convincing the lesser breeds! God created Britannia to rule.'

'What about the suppression of all political opposition? What about the Communists?'

'In Germany the word "Communist" is synonymous with "Jew". All that anti-Bolshevik propaganda after the last war was particularly effective here. It reinforced anti-Semitism.'

'And Germans believed concentration camps were the answer?' I prompted.

She shrugged. 'I suppose so — much as the British and Americans believe that prisons restrain criminals, put them where they can do no harm. By the time the truth about the concentration camps leaked out it was too late. The country was by then completely dominated by the terror machine it had licensed Hitler to build.'

'Then the truth did leak out?'

'To some. My husband was one who learned what was really going on. He became very neurotic, very depressed. Also he realised that Hitler was headed for war. Then in 1942 he was called up for military service. I think that saved him from arrest because he was becoming more and more outspoken.'

After war broke out, Frau Schreiner found a job as a radio monitor in the Foreign Office. She took stenographic notes and translated British and American broadsheets. She and her husband had never been politically active and the Gestapo paid them no attention. Her friends were tactful about her English birth.

War came as a shattering shock to the average German. From that moment, she asserted, Hitler lost his Godhead, but national emergency gave him a chance to double and redouble the power of the Gestapo. Most Germans thought Hitler had blundered when he ordered the invasion of Poland.

However, the victories of 1940 relieved the first fears. To the amazement and joy of the nation Hitler seemed to be getting away with a gamble that had seemed destined to bring only bloodshed and ruin. Reaction was ecstatic. Men who had never before spoken more than a formal word of allegiance now shouted the Führer's praises.

Then? Decline — faster and faster, blacker and blacker. The British fought on. The promised invasion of England fizzled out. More and more bombers came over German cities in spite of Goering's boasts. Hope had revived a little in 1941 when Rommel stabilised the position in the Western Desert but the attack upon Russia followed almost immediately.

'When the attack upon Russia began,' Frau Schreiner declared, 'we knew Hitler had gone mad. You have no idea how Germans fear Russians. Even those spectacular early advances didn't boost moral much — not among thinking people. Even when the armies were at the gates of Moscow there was no feeling of victory in the air. You see, by this time the public just didn't believe a word that was told them any more. My charwoman used to say the only thing you could believe in the newspapers was the date.'

This was the only point on which Frau Schreiner's account of German wartime morale substantially disagreed with accounts other people told me. They said that despair of winning did not come so soon. Some placed it as late as the Salerno landings. Many thought a stalemate, a negotiated peace, was possible until the Normandy invasion.

The fanatics might still have believed in ultimate victory, but there weren't many genuine fanatics left in the civilian population. They were all in the SS. They had been mobilised and used long before.

Stalingrad simply drove home another nail into the coffin of German hopes. Air raids grew heavier and heavier, the reaction to them was not so much fear as hate and desperation. So far, the nation had not really felt the pinch of fighting a losing war but now serious food and clothing shortages occurred and the plunge into the abyss of hopelessness accelerated. People retreated into themselves, busied themselves with tiny problems of personal survival and pleasure. Even casualties couldn't hurt them any more.

There were now no illusions about concentration camps. The final round-up of Jews by the SS in 1944 was something which horrified even anti-Semites of the older generation. Jews were seized in thousands and shipped off for extermination. Jewish children were left to starve and die in the bomb-shattered ghettoes and none dared help them.

'You ask me why none dared help them,' said Frau Schreiner bitterly. 'Well, I'll tell you. A friend of mine, a woman with no Jewish blood, one day watched SS men loading Jews into a truck to be taken away. They clung to their children, but the SS men tore them away from their parents. The children screamed with terror, and wept. My friend put her hand over her eyes and burst into tears. An SS man saw her and said, "You, you mushy bitch, come along too." They took her and I never saw her again.'

'How do you know that happened?' I asked.

'Because there was another woman with my friend — who did not cover her face and weep.'

Frau Schreiner remained at the Foreign Office until the middle of February. She then obtained permission to join her two children at Bad Nauheim. Her account of conditions in the capital was spiritless, without emotion.

'Large sections of the city burned and burned again,' she said. 'People got over being afraid. They became fatalistic, indifferent. One night when I was walking home the sparks from fires in the Charlottenburg district were so thick my fur coat caught alight.'

Her further comment on morale: 'There was no disorder. Bread queues were quiet. The Germans accepted discipline first because they like it, then because they were afraid to rebel against it, then because they were just indifferent. They didn't care about living any more. They couldn't see anything to live for. They went on making the motions of living because that was easiest.'

She then described her journey to Frankfurt in a horsecar with other evacuees. It took five days. Twice American fighter planes machine-gunned the train.

The more I analysed Constance Schreiner's story and compared its generalisations with the mass of piecemeal information I had gained from other sources, the more it seemed to approximate the truth. The picture she painted was so damnably probable and understandable.

Was there really some poison in the German psyche which predisposed the nation to arrogance and brutality, predisposed it to accept criminal leadership? If one concluded that there was, was that conclusion any more rational than the belief that some poison in the psyche of Jews predisposed them to financial intrigue and usury?

Even with the stink of the concentration camps still in my nostrils, I couldn't settle for that. The elements Hitler had juggled to create Nazi Germany existed in any society. The British had their own *Herrenvolk* myth and exploited the lesser breeds self-righteously. Americans segregated Jews socially, discriminated ruthlessly against Negro and Hispanic minorities. The French and Belgians had an appalling record of cruelty to the native population in their African colonies. The Soviet Union of separate nationalities and cultures was held together only under authority usurped by hierarchs of the New Faith, Marxism, who were as merciless in their suppression of heresy as the Church of Rome had ever been in the days of the Inquisition.

Yet, now that human decency had prevailed to put down a Germany guilty of even greater inhumanities in pursuit of self-interest, could the same human decency prevail and win the peace?

Chapter 17

In the months following the Rheims surrender very few people working in the Military Government could find time or energy to reflect on the long-term future of the dismembered nation whose day-to-day affairs they were required to direct. They were far too busy making ad hoc decisions and attempting to implement them.

But in one area meeting the needs of the moment was not enough. Some sort of rational, ongoing arrangement had to be made for the education of millions of children of school age, an education that must not perpetuate the corrupt philosophy of Nazism.

Typically, the theorists of Western democracy addressed the problem with more righteous zeal than horse sense. No tainted word or phrase should remain in the textbooks used by German schools they declared. The schools must stay closed pending a complete purge of educational literature.

The Russians were far more realistic — at least in Berlin. Even before the western Allies took over their zones they encouraged the reopening of primary schools in the least mauled suburbs, employing teachers with no notable track record as Nazi activists. They could give their pupils a grounding in the three Rs without using textbooks at all and they would hardly be reckless enough to conduct lessons in Nazi mythology on the side. West of the Elbe the reopening of schools was delayed for months.

Obviously the effective re-education of German youth, as distinct from its elementary schooling, would depend on the measures taken to counter Nazi indoctrination. Were the minds of older children and adolescents *permanently* twisted?

I had heard a great deal of talk about the 'Werewolf' organisation in the Third Reich's dying days. Goebbels boasted that a partisan army, recruited from the ranks of the Hitler Youth and exemplifying the 'invincible' spirit of the *Herrenvolk* would make foreign occupation of the Fatherland impossible. In the early days of the occupation of Bavaria a few defiant youngsters caused inconvenience to the invaders by cutting field telephone wires, planting booby traps, and daubing slogans on walls at night, but there was little evidence that a resistance movement of any consequence would grow.

However, in some districts Hitler Youth had been mobilised as auxiliaries of the Wehrmacht and *Volkssturm*, and the Americans rounded up these cadres and put them out of harm's way behind wire until the occupation was consolidated.

I visited one such compound in the country south of Munich where several hundred boys between the ages of eleven and fifteen were interned. They were living in bivouacs in an open field on near-starvation rations because of acute supply difficulties, and were eking out their daily meal by collecting and cooking edible grasses and weeds. Their behaviour was orderly. They gave no trouble to the soldiers guarding them. Like good Germans they obeyed orders, but with a dignity that most of their elders might well have emulated. They were mentally alert, reconciled to their present situation, but desperately curious about their future.

One boy asked me if it was true that they would be taken away and put to work rebuilding the cities destroyed by the Luftwaffe. I replied that I didn't think so but, supposing it were true, did he think it would be fair?

'Yes,' he said without hesitation, 'Germany lost the war. If Germany had won, we would have thought it fair to make prisoners of war rebuild our cities.'

The notes of another interview:

Q: *What do you think about the Führer now?*

A: (from a group leader aged fourteen years and eight months): The Führer deceived us. He promised victory.

Q: *Then you think the Führer was a bad man?*

A: Perhaps. I don't know — but he was wrong.

Q: *Then you think he was wrong because he failed. Could he not have been right, and also have failed?*

A: I don't understand. Please?

Q: *Do you go to church?*

A: Yes. My father and mother made me go to church.

Q: *Do you believe in God?*

A: Yes.

Q: *Do you believe in Jesus Christ?*

A: I don't know.

Q: *But you know the story of Jesus Christ?*

A: Yes, of course.

Q: *Would you say Jesus Christ was wrong because the Romans took him and crucified him?*

A: No. No, not wrong because of that.

Q: *How was he wrong then?*

A: People still don't live as he told them to live. They can't.

Q: *Does that make him wrong?*

A: No, I suppose not. But he didn't succeed.

Q: *Do you mean you think the Führer was like Jesus? He was right but he did not succeed?*

A: No, I don't think that. I think the Führer was right once, but not after he went to war. The war was where he went wrong.

Q: *Do all you boys think that?*

A: Yes, most of us think that.

Like their elders, Hitler Youth saw failure as Hitler's unforgivable sin.

Anglo-American preoccupation with the problems of how best to 're-educate' young Nazis diminished when the Soviet's plan to take out insurance against a resurgence of German militarism became clear. By unilateral decision of the Kremlin the defeated nation was to be politically partitioned and economically castrated. East Germany and the Balkan States liberated by the Red Army were to exist only as vassals of Moscow — a vast geographical buffer against aggression from the West, a shield against any action the paladins of free enterprise might take to 'kick the shit out of the Commies' when a favourable opportunity occurred again.

There could be no doubt Eastern Europe would for the foreseeable future be dominated by totalitarian Communism and live with the social and economic consequences. In due course Marxist doctrine would replace Nazi doctrine in the schoolbooks. But would Marxism have a more permanent influence than Nazism on the minds of the coming generation?

Committed, in their rhetoric at least, to the proposition that all nations should have the right of political self-determination, the Americans decided that the seeds of democracy might germinate most readily among adult adherents of the Roman Catholic faith in Bavaria. The province had been the cradle of Nazism, but the Church had retained considerable influence there under the leadership of the redoubtable prelate and politician, Cardinal Faulhaber.

Faulhaber's career in politics had suffered puzzling vicissitudes but he consistently maintained an uncompromising hostility to Communism. Until 1933 his palace had been the real headquarters of the Bavarian People's Party, theoretically in opposition to the National Socialists, but willing to make a marriage of convenience with any other party pledged to fight the Communists.

After the Nazi coup, the Bavarian People's Party was dissolved, but many of its prominent members held responsible posts under the new government.

The Cardinal's Palace forebore any overt criticism of Hitler's policies until they showed trends which were grossly anticlerical. Then Faulhaber himself and several of his bishops expressed some candid, if carefully worded, comments on moral aspects of the Führer's excesses. They dared to do so because they knew that even Hitler would be unwilling to provoke by reprisal the outright hostility of the Vatican.

Anaemic though the Cardinal's opposition to Hitler might seem, it was the straw for which the Americans groped most hopefully when they assumed the responsibility of occupation and it was not by chance that a large proportion of officers assigned to military government duties in Bavaria were themselves Roman Catholics. It was assumed that they could understand and live with the devious political techniques of the Holy See. But uncharted rocks lay ahead.

The first military governor of Bavaria was a suave Irish-American politician, Colonel Charles Keegan, who made the mistake of allying himself with Faulhaber's Palace too hastily. Like his colleagues elsewhere in Germany, he found that he could not do without Nazi help in getting the province on its feet again. Even before the end of May he appointed Fritz Schaffer, a 57-year-old lawyer and ex-chairman of the Bavarian People's Party, as temporary Minister-President of a hastily cobbled-up provincial administration.

Keegan's team faced enormous difficulties organising food supplies and coopted the services of a man named Hans Rottengruber, who had previously held a senior position in the Nazi food distribution office at Munich and who, presumably, had been a Party faithful.

Five million refugees from other parts of Germany had by now swelled the population of Bavaria to between eleven and twelve million, and even if basic diet was reduced to 1100 calories a day — roughly one third of normal nutritional requirements — famine could be avoided only by importing and distributing 25 000 tons of grain before harvest.

The Military Government was in desperate need of a diligent and efficient organiser who understood the local food distribution system. Yet Rottengruber's appointment raised a howl of outrage from the purists in Keegan's special screening branch whose duty was to sniff out lesser war criminals.

'This man is a proved Nazi and it is intolerable that he should be permitted to occupy a position of authority,' they declared. 'Remember Buchenwald, remember Belsen!'

Keegan's officer in charge of food procurement, a Texan, said to me: 'I don't care what they say about the man's politics. He's intelligent, obliging and frank — a fine Catholic gentleman into the bargain. I can't do without him.'

The row about Rottengruber leaked, of course, to the American press. Sigrid Schultz, noted Germanophobe of the *Chicago Tribune*, and Victor Bernstein, a respected Jewish commentator for *PM*, set out to break Keegan. Miss Schultz confined herself to the more lurid and biting type of article alleging that military government in Bavaria was handling war criminals with kid gloves. Bernstein attacked Keegan's administration on the ground that the Bavarian Catholics had always ranged themselves on the side of reaction and that the People's Party had nurtured the powerful banker, Adolf Muller, who in the early days had often held the fate of the National Socialists in his hands, but refrained from breaking them because they were the prime enemies of Communism.

In the end, Keegan was appointed to other duties, and Minister-President Schaffer was discredited.

Conclusion

Towards the end of August I obtained permission to travel with a squadron of reconnaissance aircraft assigned to survey and evaluate the effect of Allied strategic bombing on German heavy industry. The crews were quartered in a mansion on the outskirts of Munich owned by the infamous Dr Robert Ley, Hitler's labour minister. They flew C47 planes which, in addition to elaborate photographic equipment, carried jeeps as land transport for intelligence officers whose job was to trace and question factory executives who had survived the raids.

The analysis of data obtained on the survey, which covered every major industrial city in central and western Germany, was still on the classified documents list at the end of the year, but the snap verdict of the observers was that even the most intensive bombing had never managed to knock out key industries permanently. Heavy machinery which escaped a direct hit had been repaired and put back into service even when the buildings housing it had been demolished by fire or blast. Production was interrupted but usually resumed in a matter of days.

Similarly, the morale of civilian workers had stood up well. The RAF's night attacks of saturation bombing devastated residential areas but did little irreparable damage to factories. Anger and hatred of the 'terror fliers' increased the will to resist far more than fear softened it.

The bird's-eye view I obtained of the results of thousands of bomber raids increased my understanding of the term 'total war'. Total war was war waged between total populations. It did not and could not differentiate between combatants and noncombatants. Any talk about chivalrously sparing women, children and old people was so much hypocritical hogwash.

The news that the Americans had dropped atomic bombs on Hiroshima and Nagasaki came through while I was still with the survey squadron. No one expressed much surprise or concern about the morality of employing super-bombs to wipe out whole cities with a single detonation.

One pilot commented: 'Those Nips were goddamn lucky. They got what they had coming to them in one big dose, instead of having it doled out to them in small doses spread over years. Getting hit by a split atom can't be worse than getting sucked into a firestorm like in Hamburg or Dresden — or getting frizzled up by Napon in a bunker on the Siegfried Line.'

There had been speculation for several months about Hitler's boast that he had a secret weapon in his armoury that would assure ultimate victory. The possibility of perfecting a super-explosive would account for the priority given by the Nazis to the development of the V–1 'doodle bugs' and the V–2 rockets which could not be targeted accurately enough to do much critical damage with ordinary warheads. Now it looked as if Allied scientists had beaten their German adversaries in a race to devise a revolutionary method of delivering death and destruction.

By now desensitised by continuous proximity to death and destruction delivered by old methods, I did not at first appreciate the long-term significance of the attacks on Hiroshima and Nagasaki. Only after the precipitate surrender of Japan and the release of details which revealed the incredible power of atomic weapons, did I realise that henceforward war could have a new dimension.

Since photographing and raking through the wreckage of German cities seemed unlikely to produce much copy of interest to the newspapers I worked for, I took a short leave in

England, then flew to Nuremberg to cover preparations for the forthcoming trial of the top Nazis who had been unable to hide in their own country or, as many did, escape abroad. They were to be arraigned for 'war crimes' and/or 'crimes against humanity'. The legalistic distinction seemed to me to be an absurd quibble and the proceeding in the sombrely ornate Palace of Justice an unpleasant caricature of the processes of civilised justice.

From the outset it was clear that the 'trials' could have no more moral or judicial status than any trial by kangaroo court in the backwoods of Tennessee. The men in the dock were already condemned. They were self-confessed members of, or executive agents for, an evil regime which had been destroyed only at the cost of millions of lives. There could be no reasonable doubt about their guilt, but they were being ceremoniously paraded in a carnival of retribution as repulsive in its conception as a suggestion made by Moscow Radio: that Hitler if captured should be put in a cage and carried around the country so that people could mock and revile him!

This public vivisection of Nazi felons might expose the depravity of their motives, but neither that nor the proclamation of the penalties imposed on them, would deter criminal politicians and bureaucrats from evil-doing in the future any more than hanging, drawing or quartering on the public gallows had deterred psychopaths from committing atrocious acts in the past.

Having sacrificed so many hapless human beings to put down a rogue nation, the victors could hardly have moral scruples about inflicting capital punishment on the men who had led it into roguery. So why preface the executions with rites so inherently hypocritical that they must surely be adjudged contemptible showmanship in years to come?

My return to Nuremberg was a professional mistake. I found that I had no heart to describe the spectacle of the fat man, Goering, deprived of the wherewithal to hold up his trousers in case he should try to hang himself with belt or braces or the antics of the crazy Hess; or to record the fact that

Ley complained his meals were monotonous; or that the dock could hold twenty murderers at one time.

I applied to London for reassignment and, while awaiting movement orders, spent a good deal of time visiting a compound for Russian DPs near Ansbach, some twenty miles south-west of the city. Neither at Chemnitz nor in Berlin had I had much contact with Russians, other than in 'convivial' encounters in the Kurfurstendamm nightclubs or on stiffly official occasions at the Kommandantura.

Most of the Ansbach internees were POWs captured on the southern front in 1943 or civilians rounded up and transported to work on Bavarian farms. They included a number of young women who had been employed as domestic servants in the country houses to which wealthy industrialists had evacuated their families when the bombing of the Ruhr intensified.

These Russians were lucky in that their German masters had worked them hard but treated them tolerably well. But, for some four or five months after their liberation by the Americans, they were still waiting for the Soviet authorities to make arrangements for their repatriation.

The camp leader, Yuri Hrushkovsky, told me he had been a lecturer in European languages at the University of Odessa until called up for military service. Eventually he had been given rank as a political commissar and charged with the responsibility of keeping his infantry unit ideologically pure.

More than two years behind wire must have blunted the young commissar's missionary zeal. He spoke English fluently but in several conversations on political topics I heard no reference to 'running dogs of Capitalism' or 'Fascist-Imperialist lackeys'. Indeed, he seemed less interested in putting the Marxist point of view than in informing himself of what had been going on in the world since the Nazis put him in the bag.

When I paid my first visit to the camp in company with an official of the International Red Cross, Yuri was polite but reserved. He showed us around the dormitory huts, the mess, the kitchen and the sick bay, all of which were scrupulously clean. He insisted that we inspect the bathhouse, laundry and deep-pit latrines, amenities of which he was obviously proud. Unlike most refugee camps, this one was free of typhus, cholera and dysentery and its inhabitants, unlike most of their compatriots patrolling the Soviet Zone in Berlin, looked mentally alert and passably cheerful.

His big problem as leader, Yuri said, was to devise ways to combat boredom. Physical recreation was necessarily restricted by the 1100 calories a day but every encouragement was given to those who could organise or perform in choral concerts or variety shows. Study circles led by prisoners who had attended universities before the war were well attended. Chess and woodcarving were popular pastimes. Lack of reading matter of any kind was a great hardship for the better educated.

On my second visit to the compound I carried a bundle of American newspapers and illustrated magazines salvaged from the correspondents' quarters in a Nuremberg hotel — and half-a-dozen cartons of cigarettes purchased from the PX. I apologised for my failure to find anything printed in Russian.

Yuri's eyes sparkled with delight. He handled well-thumbed copies of *Time, Life* and *Saturday Evening Post*, with something approaching reverence. Some of his people had learned English at school, he said, and could translate the most interesting news items and articles to others of their group. I could not have brought a gift that would be more appreciated.

A little embarrassed by the man's show of gratitude, I muttered something about doing better the next time I passed this way. His eyes narrowed and met mine. 'Then you will come to see us again?' he asked.

'Sure thing,' I said, 'if you don't object. As a matter of fact, you're doing such a good job here, I'd like to write an article about this camp.'

He gave a small, indifferent shrug. 'You are very welcome,' he said. 'Would it be an inconvenience for you to come in the evening?'

'Of course not,' I replied. 'But why?'

He looked a little shifty. 'If you could come in the evening, perhaps I could persuade you to talk to a select group of our young people interested in geography — to tell them about life in your homeland, Australia.'

'But, good God, Yuri,' I objected, 'I don't speak a word of Russian and my German is pretty primitive. How many of the audience would understand what I had to say?'

'There are several girls here who speak English,' he said. 'They could interpret. I could myself, but if I am present then perhaps discussion will be less free. You understand? You would not have to prepare a lecture — just answer the questions put to you.'

The prospect of being quizzed by a team of young Russians about life in Australia was less than exhilarating, but Yuri Hrushkovsky was so diffidently importunate that I hadn't the heart to refuse him.

The 'select group' turned out to number about a hundred, crammed into a dilapidated quonset hut which could have accommodated about half the number comfortably. I answered questions non-stop for more than two hours — questions which covered every conceivable aspect of life in the mysterious continent of bounding kangaroos, furred animals with ducks' bills which lived underwater and laid eggs, and pygmy bears which carried their young on their backs like monkeys and ate nothing but gum leaves.

Was it true that the whole interior of the country was desert? How high were the mountains? How large were the cities? How much were industrial workers paid and did they have production quotas to meet? Was the land worked by freeholders or tenant farmers? What were the staple foods? Climate…terrain…literature and the arts…popular sports… schools…hospitals…?

Probably the barrage of questions was orchestrated by Yuri or his group leader. I was not asked a single question about Australia's political system, or what degree of autonomy it enjoyed as a British Dominion. But the audience was genuinely interested, almost fiercely attentive, when the interpreter, a handsome, dark-haired woman in her twenties who spoke English in an odd, ventriloquial pitch of voice gave the Russian version of my replies.

At the end of the performance a rather melancholy young man rose to his feet and made a short speech of thanks which needed no translation. Applause was thunderous, but when it subsided the speaker added a few words which evoked a roar of laughter and more handclapping.

'What did he say?' I asked.

The dark-haired interpreter said in her shrill English, 'He says that he and his comrades would like to visit your country and see with their own eyes the fish with fur.'

Subsequent sessions with Yuri and the half-dozen or so English-speakers he encouraged to join in the conversation were more relaxed and, to me, informative. No one wished to discuss their experiences during the war. The war was history. It was more stimulating to speculate about the postwar world. The candour with which members of the group expressed diverse views on contentious subjects surprised me. One young woman said she felt she needed religion to sustain her, and would like to be received into the Roman Catholic faith rather than the Russian Orthodox Church. Comrade Commissar Hrushkovsky didn't bat an eyelid. A student from Odessa University who said he wished to graduate in agricultural science after he returned home, confessed his doubt that collective farms in the USSR would ever succeed because they offered the peasantry no incentive to work hard. Comrade Commissar Hrushkovsky commented mildly that education would in time alter the attitude of rural workers.

Several of the periodicals I had brought to the camp contained articles about the atomic bombs dropped on Japan. I asked if anyone had read them and, if so, what were their thoughts. There were five or six in the group at the time. There was an embarrassed silence. Yuri answered.

'I have discussed it with my comrades,' he said stiffly. 'We do not believe that the Russian people will surrender if such a weapon is used against them. But perhaps this new explosive will serve the cause of peace. The damage it has done in Japan may convince the leaders of nations that they have much more to gain from preventing a war than from winning it. The danger is that fear does not restrain madmen whose only thirst is for power.

Three days later I paid a farewell call on the Ansbach camp. It was a pitch-dark, bitterly cold night. Yuri Hrushkovsky walked beside me to the compound gates. 'So you are going home at last, my friend,' he said. 'I envy you. What will you do when you arrive?'

'Take a vacation with my wife and children I hope — then back to my work.'

'I envy you. I have no wife and children, but I too will have a vacation.'

'Good for you,' I said. 'Where?'

He dropped his voice as if afraid of being overheard. 'In a political re-education centre.'

When I was sure I had my voice under control I said: 'I see. What will you do afterwards, Yuri?'

'I will be directed to suitable employment. Perhaps to teaching again, helping to heal Russia's wounds and build a socialist state prosperous enough to afford the freedom you already enjoy in your country. Here in Europe freedom is very expensive.'

We shook hands.

'Goodbye and good luck, Yuri,' I said. 'Take care.'

He chuckled.

'You too, comrade,' he said. 'You, too, take care.'

My journey as a civilian observer with the armies that invaded and occupied Germany in 1945 lasted ten months. But I am conscious of how little one pair of eyes could see and one set of brains could understand of the action on so vast a battlefield.

What I did see and understand makes me chary of regarding the outcome as a triumph of good over evil.

The majority of the men and women who fought and died — and killed — to crush Hitler's Third Reich believed in the justice of their cause. They might not have believed they were creating 'a world fit for heroes to live in', or that they were fighting a 'war to end wars', but they did at least hope that if they won, the postwar world would be one in which human decency and human dignity could survive.

Those who stayed on with the armies of occupation to salvage what could be salvaged from the wreckage of a nation dismembered by brute force, and if possible trace the origins and course of the disease that had justified its destruction, must have been sobered by an inescapable conclusion. Susceptibility to Nazism is not peculiar to people of Teutonic stock. The virus lies dormant in all egocentric societies of whatever ethnic derivation. It proliferates under stress — particularly under the sort of stress caused by economic depression and vacillation in political leadership. The first symptom is the growth of rabid nationalism; the next, surrender to demagogy and acceptance of the proposition that dictatorship is the only cure for disunity and inefficient government. Submission to a fear-machine designed to silence the voice of dissident minorities is the final, fatal phase of a cancer that could destroy the forms of civilisation evolved by democracy.

In the armies which liberated the concentration camps there were many then who in other circumstances might well have been storm-troopers, and the sort of moral cretins who nurture ancient hatreds and commit atrocities in the name of patriotism or religious conviction. Such people can be found in any army — or in any cheering, chanting mob. Race has nothing to do with it. Some of the most inhuman cruelties in the camps, and in towns and villages overrun by prisoners liberated from the camps, were perpetrated by non-Germans — by renegade Frenchmen, Poles, Czechs, Hungarians, Britons and Americans.

Yet Germany must still bear the burden of collective guilt because, under Hitler, its freely chosen and acclaimed leader, it tolerated the recruitment of evil men as the bodyguard of the even more evil men who had seized power.

Yes, Yuri Hrushkovsky — we must both take care.

INTRODUCTION TO 1945 MANUSCRIPT

Readers who prefer to take their ration of history in the clearly labelled, predigested form are so likely to be affronted by this book that I hasten to evoke the golden rule of war reporting: dig a nice, deep hole before the shooting starts. This book is not a history of the invasion of Germany from the west. I deny that it even faintly resembles a history of the invasion of Germany from the west. Any man who claims he can write such a history, confining himself wholly or substantially to what he saw for himself, is either a great egotist or a great liar — or both. At most, *Conquerors' Road* rates classification as 'source material'.

Nevertheless, in writing it I have been moved by something more than the spirit of anecdotage. The months of 1945 during which Germany was invaded, conquered and occupied by the Allied armies were climatic months in a great and tragic period of human history. I am conscious and proud of the privilege I enjoyed during those months as a war correspondent attached to General Eisenhower's armies. I felt then, as I feel now, that the privilege carried with it a grave responsibility: that of seeking out the truth, recognising it, and telling as much of it as could be told without giving aid and comfort to the enemy.

Today, however, there is no enemy to aid and comfort, and I believe that the sooner the whole truth is assembled and studied, and its lessons digested, the better it will be for humanity. *Conquerors' Road* is one man's contribution to the mosaic of the whole truth — offered with full realisation of its inadequacy and fallibility but with confidence that it is truth told as well as I can tell it.

One more explanation. Any witness of great events who wishes to give evidence before the courts of the historians cannot hope to record everything he saw. He must accept responsibility for selecting from the field of his observation that which he believes important and pertinent. He must also give his testimony some unity and form. I have tried to do this by answering the following self-posed questions:

- What did you see of actual military operations during the invasion of Germany and what is your comment on what you saw ?
- Putting aside matters of 'common knowledge' and propaganda, what did you see inside Germany which seemed to justify the defeat and dismemberment of the Third Reich?
- Again without prejudice, what measures did you see taken by the victorious Powers in Germany with the object of preventing future wars, and did those measures appear to you to be rightly directed and adequate?

The first questions I have answered in Part 1, 'Execution', the second in Part 2, 'Autopsy', and the third in Part 3, 'Burial'. [*This structure was abandoned during White's 1983 revisions.*]

The adoption of this method made it necessary to abandon any effort to preserve chronological continuity. Experiences relevant to those questions overlapped and doubled back on themselves repeatedly. The people who finish this book will, therefore, be the people who read to know what happened, not those who read to know

O.E.W.
London, November 1945

WHITE'S DISPATCH ON BUCHENWALD, THE *COURIER-MAIL*, BRISBANE, 18 APRIL 1945

Invaders Rip Veil From Nazi Horrors

April 17. Dismemberment of Germany by invasion armies in the last week or ten days has disclosed moral debasement which has destroyed the nation's soul as surely as bombers, guns, and tanks have destroyed its physical entity.

We are in the heart of Germany, in a diseased nation. We are in the concentration camp country. Today I've seen the Buchenwald, and moved among its living dead. I cannot now nor ever will be able to write objectively of what I have seen. One cannot observe war for three-and-a-half years as a newspaperman and remain either sentimentalist or supersensitive about spectacles of human suffering. Yet what I saw today moved me to physical illness.

It moved me to the conviction that never again can civilisation trust the German people as they are to determine their own social and political destiny.

Before that the civilised world must be assured — more, convinced by unchallengeable proofs — that the Germans have been severed completely from the inheritance of a past which is not only their shame, but the shame of all humanity.

This morning I left the city of Weimar, the beloved home of Goethe, Schiller, and Liszt, and drove three miles through forests and fields beautiful with spring.

I came to a fence of barbed wire, and an entrance lodge of brown wood, over which a great black flag hung limply on a pole.

This, they told me, was the Buchenwald — the deepest pit of the hell Hitler has dug.

I said to myself: 'One more concentration camp. Tighten up your guts. Get ready to look at torture hooks and corpses.'

They told me that once there were 50 000 people here, but now there were only 20 000. I went through the iron gates, looking at people who walked about on concrete, grave courtyards. Most of them showed signs of slow starvation. They were clad in ragged ugly prison suits. They were unshaven. The lines on their faces were lines etched there by long suffering and the death of hope. They wore little coloured badges to indicate the nature of their 'offence' and their nationality.

For six weeks now I have been seeing people like these on the roads all through Germany. I have been answering their salutes until my arms tired and their smiles until my answering smile became meaningless.

These were the same slaves — not yet quite free, and a little hungrier — a little uglier, more brutalised.

Doctor Hugo Mortelmans, lecturer in pathology at Antwerp Medical School, a small, round-faced man with blank bright eyes, came forward and offered himself as guide and interpreter. He had been taken by the Gestapo because of his resistance activities, and given employment in the SS 'Department of Histology'.

First he led the way to a concrete court where the day's dead were being loaded into an iron-sided truck. There were about 100 blue-white stiff bodies, with shaven skulls and the purple bruises of beatings still on their skins. They were most horribly emaciated from starvation and disease. Atop of them was the limp, fat corpse of an SS man who hanged himself in a cell last night.

We went to the crematorium where six furnaces still contained the blackened frames of what once were men. Above the door was a verse beginning:

'Worms shall not devour me, but flames consume this body. I always loved the heat and light…'

Garrotters' Room Of Death

We descended to the death-room in the basement, containing holes with 30 hooks upon which men had been garrotted.

The holes had been hastily plastered up and whitewashed, in a vain effort to conceal the room's purpose. An attendant showed me a club with which those who did not die quickly enough had their brains beaten out. Dr. Mortelmans said he believed that between 30 and 40 Allied airmen had been executed.

It was estimated that 48 000 executions took place in five years.

From this place we were taken to the SS museum of pathology, where magnificently prepared sections of diseased organs of the human body were displayed.

Forced Research

Here Dr. Mark Klein, professor of Histology in Strasbourg University, who had been interned in Buchenwald camp since May 5, 1944, said that he had been forced to work preparing sections. So many cases of all kinds of disease in all stages, were available as material that the work done here was of scientific value.

Other such work also done here was of no scientific value whatever. It was indulged in solely to satisfy the sadistic mania of those in control.

Dr. Klein produced sections of human skin bearing elaborate tattoo marks, which, he said, were prepared and preserved by a German doctor, who had written and published a paper about them.

Dr. Klein produced two human heads on wooden mounts, and explained that the technician who prepared them had carefully followed the shrinking process of the Jivaro Indians of South America. They were the heads of Poles or Russians.

The heads were so perfectly preserved that they still bore the expression the men died with.

I was taken to 'Block 50' — the department of bacteriology, where a slave scientist, Professor Maurice Suard, of Angers medical school, explained the work done. Their chief task had been the development of anti-typhus serum. After experiments on animals, Nazi physicians had deliberately inoculated healthy prisoners with typhus virus, to observe the course of the disease and the efficacy of various sera.

Professor Suard said that batches of 40 to 50 prisoners had been executed by toxic injections.

He demonstrated the excellent scientific equipment of the block, and said that the work undertaken there was of objective scientific value, but that the experiments had been undertaken with complete disregard of human life and suffering, and countless prisoners had been murdered by Nazi scientists in their experiments.

Slave scientists had not been required to make these experiments. They were employed solely to prepare sera, to do work in which there was danger of infection, of which the Germans were almost ludicrously afraid, and to keep records which were sent to Berlin.

Filthy Bunks

Dr Joseph Brau, a physician from Coulommiers, who is now acting chief physician of all prisoners remaining in the camp, conducted me to the quarters of the Poles and Russians. I first inspected the barracks of 'normal' prisoners.

They showed advanced malnutrition and were sleeping or lying in filthy three-tier bunks.

Ten men were in each compartment of the hut, which was swarming with vermin. All the occupants were suffering from dysentery. Many of the men were obviously insane.

As the party walked by the hut and British uniforms were recognised a low, growling noise broke out. I did not recognise that this was a kind of applause until someone started hand-clapping.

Men crawled weakly from their bunks, stood at attention, and saluted.

Children In Jungle Of Suffering

Among the prisoners were children aged 11 and 12. Dr Brau said that mostly children were sent to gas chambers.

One man concealed his son in this jungle of indescribable suffering for three years. We saw the child. He was five years old, and tolerably nourished. His father was washing his hands, which were delicately formed.

Dr. Brau then conducted me to the 'sick house'. I cannot picture for you what I saw there.

I can only say that here the dead walked or stood stark naked outside in the sun, shivering uncontrollable rigours, or lay in the filth of their diseases.

I can only say that their voices sounded like wind in a dark, deep place; that the image of their eyes and their teeth as they smiled will, until the day of my death, remain my life's most terrible recollection.

I said to Dr. Brau: 'The only humane thing the Germans have done here they did when they strangled them.'

He replied: 'That is true.'

After this inspection I did not go to the brothel kept by the guards for prisoners who had money, and to which women were assigned as a final punishment.

I went back to the town where Goethe, Schiller, and Liszt lived and worked.

In a recent dispatch I said that the people who make the peace settlement with Germany should, before making it, see for themselves the destruction of Germany's material assets before speaking of reparations. I implied what I still believe to be true — that Germany will be unable to make material reparation.

To that I would add that only God is powerful enough to exact spiritual reparation for what has happened in such camps as Buchenwald.

But the men who make peace should be required also to see such camps, and be made to take an oath before mankind to make and keep the kind of peace in which never again will any nation in the human family be permitted the power to debase itself to such a level of bestiality as has Germany in the years between 1933 and 1945.

It may be true that 99 per cent of Germans did not know what was going on, but it is certainly true that they did not know, because they had not the guts to find out, much less to do anything about it.

THE ORGANISATION OF SLAVE LABOUR: EXTRACT FROM UNREVISED 1945 MANUSCRIPT

Out of scores of such glimpsed scenes on the roads of Germany, one came at last to build up a picture of enormous confusion and drama; some conception of what humanity is really like when its social organisation, even a slave organisation, has collapsed. But the picture was still impersonal and its motivation was still obscure. These people on the roads of Germany were still so alien to most of us that they might almost have been of another species. They were the living debris of a tremendous social convulsion, they were at first no more real than the characters in a motion picture drama. Only when they stopped being a sort of pageant of imponderable events, when one got to know some of them as individuals, was it possible to feel the weight of human tragedy they bore on their bent shoulders as they marched out.

It is improbable that any really accurate account will ever be given of the number of foreigners brought willingly or forcibly into Germany to hew the wood and draw the water while the master race got on with the fighting.

A month after the Rheims surrender the displaced persons division of the Allied Military Government at Frankfurt issued a statement that the number then registered exceeded five million. After the British and American forces moved into Berlin, Dr. Ferdinand Friedensburg, director of the German Institute of Economic Research, a man who had access to official statistics until the collapse, told me that more than ten million foreigners had worked for the Reich.

'Judged by absolute standards,' he said, 'it was uneconomical labour. Half as many well men might have done twice the work, but Germany's commitment to the war was total. Ten million slave workers were one of the main reasons why we were able to carry on so long.'

The slave workers fell into four classes of origin: war prisoners, civilian draftees from conquered or satellite states, political prisoners on assignment from concentration camps, and 'volunteers' recruited in France, the Low Countries, and elsewhere.

They were employed in practically every type of work. There were teams of slave scientists in German laboratories, slave technicians in German aircraft and munitions factories, slave shophands and slave domestics, slave bank clerks and office workers, slaves in salt and coal mines, slaves ploughing fields, digging ditches, working timber, puddling iron, and hewing stone. There were even slave physicians and surgeons I myself saw and talked with people who had worked in every one of these jobs — and in scores more. No pair of hands was too weak or incapable to be forced to fight Nazism's battles on the home front. Where they could be obtained, young, vigorous people were preferred; but in labour camps in central Germany I saw ten-year-old children who had been forced to work in the mines, and 70-year-old men who had been assigned to labour in quarries.

It is impossible to generalise about their treatment. Some were paid wages roughly the equivalent of Germans doing the same work. These were usually the volunteers, the collaborators, who worked willingly and gave no trouble. War prisoners from western nations for the most part received the standard pay set down by the Geneva Convention. Conscripts worked at 'penalty rates' and concentration camp inmates for canteen vouchers so low in value that a week's pay would not buy a meal.

Pay was never a yardstick of treatment — either in the German slave state-within-a-state, or elsewhere. At one end of the scale were people who held positions of limited responsibility in offices, warehouses or banks. They had 'behaved themselves' and were let alone. They had been docile and had enjoyed the rewards of docility.

At the other end of the scale were people who fell dead of starvation and disease at their machines; or in mines and ditches and sewers.

Two qualities Hitlerism demanded of its slaves: a strong body and a docile mind. With both they survived. Without they died.

WHITE'S DISPATCH ON SUDETEN GERMAN EXPULSION, THE *HERALD*, MELBOURNE, 19 JUNE 1945

Sudeten Germans Driven Out Of Czechoslovakia: Unwanted In Own Land

Pilsen, Czechoslovakia. Tens of thousands of Germans, dispossessed by the Czech National Committees which took over local government after the liberation, are streaming in forlorn bands through the Sudeten mountains headed for the disintegrated Reich.

They are travelling by foot or in convoys of canvas-covered ox-carts, in which are crammed a few personal belongings they have been allowed to take, and hordes of unwashed, tatterdemalion children. They are hungry, fear-haunted, hopeless — ejected violently from the country which their nation exploited, but unwanted in their own homeland.

Tens of thousands more are sitting morosely in Czech concentration camps on near-starvation rations, often without sanitation and proper shelters, awaiting almost indifferently for the Czechs to decide what shall be done with them. At least this minority of *Herrenvolk* are suffering the fate the Germans imposed on 15 million other European nationals when they herded slave-labour bands into the Reich to serve the German war machine. Because of the isolation of the country the Czech resistance to the Germans was less active than in many other conquering countries, but now the Germans are beaten the repressed hatred of the Czechs is finding violent expression.

Innocent Suffer

In most cases, dispossession has been immediate and peremptory. First to go were Germans who openly expressed sympathy and approval of Hitler, but the purge did not stop there. Germans with 20 to 30 years' residence — even second generation Germans — are being forced to pack up and get out.

This may well be the forerunner of a great movement by the Balkan countries to settle their German minority problems by forced repatriation, affecting in all many millions. In countless cases innocent people will suffer inhuman hardship and ruin, yet it is a mere gleaning in a Europe-wide harvest of the hatred and turmoil sown by the Germans' aggression.

Object Lesson

A journey through southern Germany into Czechoslovakia is an unforgettable object lesson in the reality of the German exploitation of subject countries. Sudeten villages and towns are virtually untouched by the war. Fat-looking farm houses squat in neat fields and the people are well fed and clothed.

The Czech border is high in the mountains and once it is passed travellers are in another world. The earth is the same, but the fields and forests are untidy and tended in such a way as to wring out only an immediate return. The children are thin, dirty and in rags.

Farmhouses are tumble-down and unpainted, and the peasants are bent and knotted up with endless labour. Villages, although they are bright with Czech, Russian and American flags, have an ash-grey atmosphere of oppression and poverty.

The Germans made rural Czechoslovakia a 'truck farm' to feed the inhabitants of the industrial cities of the Reich, allotting each peasant a quota production which he must meet or be punished.

Satisfaction

The peasants are finding a savage satisfaction in the eviction of German landowners and small tradesmen, in scoring out German shop signs, notices and road signs. And consolation in a return to the attitude of militant nationalism.

The industrial position is somewhat different and is definitely more encouraging.

Cities like Pilsen and Prague are living drably on short commons, but the nation's industrial potential is damaged comparatively little by the war.

It is true that in the final days some damage was done by Allied bombing, but compared with Germany, Poland, West Russia and Italy, Czech industry got off scot-free.

The problem facing the Czechs is to persuade the rest of Europe to let them alone to work out their own destiny and, secondly, to compose the differences which have always existed between the Moravian, Bohemian, Slovakian population, and between the industrial and agrarian elements. War has only intensified those differences.

Meeting Point

At the moment though the precise intentions of the occupying Powers are not clear. Like Yugoslavia Czechoslovakia is the meeting point for two apparently inimical spheres of interest — that of Western Allies and that of Soviet Russia.

As in 1938 the Czechs themselves are really helpless. They are being allowed to play out their domestic political drama only at the sufferance of their big liberators.

Old Spectre

The centuries-old spectre which haunts the council rooms of the peacemakers is on the prowl again. Its name is 'Tension in Central Europe'.

The greatest single query in international relationships today is whether the United States and

Great Britain can manage to get along with Soviet Russia.

Here on 'neutral territory' American and Russian occupation forces impinge and their tacit sponsorship of different political philosophies clash.

Today the cities of Prague and Pilsen, indeed, the whole country, is a propagandist's paradise and an honest reporter's purgatory. It is a land of half-truths and prejudiced perceptions, of hereditary hatred and blind loyalties.

In squares and marketplaces, shabby, sharp-faced factory workers are meeting to hear speeches and cheer references to Communism and Russia. In the shops idle shopkeepers, and in the barns plundered by the Nazis, the sullen peasants mutter distrust of the Reds. In cafes and clubs, agent provocateurs whisper tales of Russian shootings, rape and loot, or of collaborationists gone unpunished, and of Fascist plots to betray the Proletariat.

Tension

There is an undercurrent of brittle tension, an atmosphere of covert struggle and manoeuvre more disquieting than any I have encountered in Europe.

'We are disappointed with liberation. Cynicism is growing again,' declared one man who dutifully told me his party's hardluck story. However questionable the rest of his tale may have been, in those two sentences he spoke something very near the truth.

The most dangerous manoeuvre of the reactionary elements is an effort to implant the idea that only the presence of American forces prevents the immediate institution of a Russian reign of terror.

There is no reign of terror in Prague or any part of Bohemia. Russians are stern realists with the collaborator and the Fascist element, but a man whose conscience is clear can go without fear.

The discipline of the Red Army is good. There is no more looting, rape or bullying than in any zone of occupation. Wild stories of brutality arise from magnification and distortion of individual instances, given verisimilitude by the Czechs' nervousness of the Russian soldiers' exuberant manners and their liking for vodka.'

One woman who told me the most hair-raising tales of Russian brutality in Prague was forced in the end to admit that the only evidence she had seen with her own eyes was drunken Russian officers firing pistols into the air or shooting at bottles.

In the field of mechanical politics there is no evidence that the Russians have determined to dictate the country's political fate by force or fait accompli.

MILITARY OCCUPATION: EXTRACT FROM UNREVISED 1945 MANUSCRIPT

In Berlin came realisation, as emotional acceptance, of the fact that the war was over. There was no foe left to defeat. Whatever happened was solely the responsibility of the victors. The enemy was now without power either to hurt others or help himself. The Third Reich no longer existed. Its every working part was smashed. No conquest had ever been more complete.

There was very little jubilation among the victorious troops. On the contrary, there was among them a profound depression, a flatness of spirit, a restlessness. Few expressed any belief that, now the joyless task of execution was finished, the world was going to be a much better or safer place to live in.

Now that peace had come, newspapers in Britain and the United States were giving prominence to discussion of the problem of convincing the German people that this time they were beaten. To most troops in Germany this seemed a queer idiocy — rather like worrying about how to convince a man of your unfriendliness after you have kicked his wife, maltreated his children, burned down his house and hit him on the head with a club. If the Germans still doubted they were beaten, they could surely never be convinced of defeat by the studied humiliations and childish disciplines devised by politicians seeking the approbation of vengeful mobs.

Many times during the war I had been conscious of my own inability as a journalist to tell the truth as clearly and forcefully as it needed to be told; and many times I had been depressed by the inadequacy of the newspaper as a vehicle for truth telling, but never before this had I been quite so bitterly aware of journalism's shortcomings — the inescapable fact that newspapers exist far more to select for their readers the news that they want to hear than to give them the news that they ought to hear. With scores of other newspapermen working in Germany after the collapse, I too received the inevitable memorandum suggesting that now this unpleasant business of killing and destroying was finished, readers would be grateful for stories emphasising the humours, the lighter side of victory.

This in a charnel house! There was no lighter side to victory. Victory weighed even heavier on the spirit than fears during conflict.

When early in the year the Americans had moved into Trier, a young major of the military government division gave a group of correspondents a clear statement of what he believed his job to be.

'As I see it,' he said, 'the Military Government is to restore and preserve order in Germany, to find and punish the guilty, to revive the moral perception of the German people, and to prevent a recurrence of German aggression.'

At the time, that seemed a simple and adequate definition of what every decent man *hoped* military government would do. They were reassuring words but, like most reassuring words, they glossed over a multitude of practical complications.

In the first place there were four military governments in Germany, not one. Between the four, no substantial agreement had ever been reached. An Englishman, an American, a Russian, a Frenchman, meant quite different things when they talked about 'order', 'guilt', 'moral perception', or 'aggression'. Even if the Powers had done what they ought to have done — reached substantial agreement on the dialectics of occupation before Germany collapsed — these aims would not have been separable. They were bound together. They often conflicted. Too close pursuit of one was inevitably to cloud perception of the rest. Nevertheless, one was always forced back to acknowledge that simplified ideal: *Restore order...punish the guilty...revive moral perception...prevent recurrence.* Only thus could victory be justified and made positive.

The first aim of military government, the restoration and preservation of order, was in itself very difficult. Enforcement of the regulations promulgated by the occupying Powers was only a first step towards it. In general, neither British, Americans nor Russians had much trouble in exacting obedience from German civilians. German civilians were only too anxious to obey. Theirs was a wordless docility of a people reduced to complete dependence. When proclamations were posted up, groups would gather about them, read slowly and carefully, disperse quickly. Then, when military government had been formally established, queues would form and wait patiently for hours for the most trivial permissions. Was it permitted to do this...do that? Was it permitted to work thus...or so? Was it permitted to visit one's uncle in the country? To seek food from friends on a nearby farm? To cut wood for fuel? To drive a horse and cart, ride a bicycle, walk to the next town? Was it permitted to resist looting by displaced persons? To draw money from the bank if the bank opened? Send a letter by hand to a friend? Buy, sell things ?

It was a macabre experience to watch these German people come to the military government inquiry desks — children, old men, women; rich, poor; fat, thin; well, ill. They came in every condition of mind, from calm fatalism to stammering terror. Sometimes there were among them individuals with a complaint or a grievance, but in the early days of occupation these were few.

The soldiers who dealt with this part of military government business were on the whole forbearing and courteous — the British and Americans, at least. Very few whom I encountered subscribed to the theory that the only good Germans were dead Germans. They were men who were in the main sensitive enough to appreciate the vastness of the tragedy that had befallen Germany. They were not harsh in manner. At best, they were sympathetic; at worst, unfriendly. They bullied very little.

Only foreign workers, recruited for service as clerks and interpreters, acted as if they had old scores to pay off. One Dutchman I remember particularly. He was a small, white-faced, round-headed fellow. He said his wife and children had been killed in the bombing of Rotterdam. He had been deported to Germany to work in a bank. I spent the best part of one morning watching him make the permission-seeking citizens of Erfurt squirm and sweat. The highlight of this grisly performance was his dealing with a woman wanting a travel permit to take her two small children to friends in the country near Herstein. She was quite obviously near nervous collapse. Her face was grey and beaded with sweat. Her hands, clutching a black leather handbag, trembled convulsively. She could barely stand. When her turn came at the desk, she made a supreme effort to control herself and to state the request clearly and rapidly. Her lips twisted into a meaningless smile. She put the bag down on the desk and leaned forward, palms flat on the wood.

The Dutchman did not look at her. He fixed his eyes on the handbag, waited for half a minute after she had finished, without speaking. Then he said softly and almost inaudibly: 'Take that filth off my desk and stand in a respectful attitude when you address me. Good. That is much better. Now tell me again what you want.'

The woman opened her mouth. No words came. The Dutchman slowly raised his eyes.

'Well?' he asked with a gently, feline smile.

The woman fainted.

'Take her out of here,' he said, still quietly, when the disturbance subsided. 'Pour some water over her.'

I asked the commanding officer of the headquarters about the Dutchman.

'He is invaluable,' he replied. 'He understands how to handle krauts and he does the work of half-a-dozen men. I hope to keep him with me.'

Nothing I could observe in Germany supported the contention that the docility of the people was a sham. Restoration and preservation of order was not complicated by the resistance of 'patriots'. In the Third Reich's dying days, Nazi leaders had boasted that a great partisan army would make occupation of the Fatherland impossible for foreigners. The great partisan army proved a myth. As far as I know, the first phase of the occupation of Germany passed without one single major act of revolt or disobedience by any organised group of Germans.

Even the Werewolf organisation, calculated to appeal to the 'invincible spirit of Nazi Youth', fizzled ignominiously. In spite of the determined efforts of a certain section of the British and American press to whip up some respect for its menacing possibilities, it was never more than a few loosely coordinated bands of youngsters whose most notable feats of sabotage were to cut telephone wires, plant a few booby traps, and daub defiant slogans on walls at night.

Vigorous action by Allied counterintelligence men may have scotched the Werewolf movement before it could really start operations. This was claimed, but it was not claimed by the counterintelligence men themselves. Most of them agree, even as late as six months after the surrender, that there was little evidence to show that Nazi organisations of any significant magnitude existed underground in defeated Germany. Whatever 'national spirit' survived in Germany, whatever potential aggressiveness it possessed, it was not identified with Nazism or Nazi doctrine. The German people as a whole were willing wholeheartedly to cooperate in the restoration and preservation of the order designed and dictated by the victors. This willingness was not based on goodwill but on dire necessity. Nazism had destroyed alternatives, and now Nazism itself was destroyed. Germans were dependent entirely upon their conquerors to restore and preserve for them that minimum of regulation without which men cannot live together.

Order, law itself, is not absolute. It has meaning only after basic material necessities of life have been provided. Order, in the long run, depends upon sewers that work, water taps that run, roofs that keep out the weather, larders with food in them. Order is productive work for men and women, means of transport and communication, education, recreation, religion, security, a state of mind. Order is civilisation itself, in which the material and non-material are inextricably bound together. Military government teams moving into the ruined cities and towns of Germany found that the provision of even temporary order was a task which, for weeks and months, excluded consideration of almost all others. The objectives of punishment, re-education and permanent settlement of the 'German problem' had, out of desperate necessity, to be shelved until the machinery of community life was restored.

This was something which two or three hundred Allied newspaper correspondents in Germany failed to explain in intelligible terms to their readers. Typically and understandably, people whose own community organisation still functioned as unnoticed as their own heartbeats could not feel that the flushing of German water closets was ultimately a more vital factor in the regulation of defeated Germany than the excision of Nazi propaganda from German schoolbooks. Only the harried men who were charged with the responsibility of meeting the threat of pestilence in near-obliterated cities could appreciate such prosaic, non-political, non-moral truth.

The principle that order could be established in Germany only on the basis of reconstruction and reorganisation of the country's material resources was capable of almost indefinite extension. It was apparent to anyone entering a ruined city that the population must be assured of food, shelter and sanitation before there was any sense in worrying over precise applications of criminal law and the protection of individual property. It was not, perhaps, so apparent to anyone entering a ruined province that a workable system for the production, distribution and exchange of essential commodities must take precedence over educational reform or the detection and punishment of minor political criminals, but it was equally true. Still less apparent was the fact that when a nation has been ruined, restoration of a tolerably balanced national economy must take precedence over any enterprise to educate its people in a positive and liberal political philosophy. In each case, the abstract factors of civilised order could only be based upon equitably and efficiently organised material factors.

Failure to put first things first was the initial failure of the Allied Military Government in Germany. The fault was not that of the Military Government executive. Most Military Government executives — among the British and Americans at least — were efficient and aware of their humanitarian responsibility. They were dealing with living human material: men, women and children who must, as one officer put it, 'be kept standing up'. They were handicapped in the job of keeping the Germans standing up by political elements in their own armies and governments which were dealing not with living human material but with abstract political ideas. This political element was not concerned with the welfare of the German people. It was concerned with satisfying the public of the victorious nations that the people of Germany were still being punished for having caused the war, and with trying to convince them that whatever happened Germany would never again be permitted enough material strength to fight again. Rehabilitation of a nation as completely desolated as Germany and its simultaneous 'punishment' were impossible. Vengeance and humanitarianism do not mix — even if the electorates of the democracies cried lustily for both, and political journalists did prodigious feats of selecting and distorting fact to convince them they were getting both.

It seemed to me that the Russians were the only victors who did not attempt to run with the hare and hunt with the hounds. From what I could see and hear, they were unconcerned with problems of 'humanitarianism' as it was defined by the British or the Americans. Nor were they concerned with vengeance for the sake of vengeance. They were the sublime egoists, the uncompromising realists. An English-speaking ordinance officer in the Kabarett der Kommiker, the candour of wine in him, told me: 'We are pledged to destroy Fascism. German Fascism is no worse than any other Fascism. The only country in the world which recognises and destroys Fascism in any disguise is Russia — but it is not a matter of nationality, you know. Nationality is not important to us. We do not hate Germans — or Italians or Chinese or Negroes. Oh no. We do not think Russians are better than other people, except perhaps that Russians have a system of government which seeks to destroy Fascism. We will make Russia strong and secure — not to impose our will on other peoples but to defend men against Fascism wherever it shows itself. Russia must first be made strong and secure. We will take in reparations from the guilty nations only what is necessary to make Russia strong and secure. That is good sense. That is logic. We have nothing against capitalist democracy, except perhaps that it turns Fascist so easily when something goes wrong with the machinery.'

In bringing order to their zone, the Russians thought and acted in terms of the mass. They did not worry about precise justice for the individual. They were chiefly concerned with making every community as near self-supporting as possible in the shortest possible time. Their first thought was to provide productive occupation for everyone capable of working. Neither in the expulsion of

Germans from areas destined for cession to Poland or Czechoslovakia, nor in reallocation of populations when a workable balance between district and district had been upset by the influx of war refugees, nor in destruction of industrial plants, were the Soviets constrained by what the British and Americans — or even the French — would call mercy. They rearranged the human herds of Soviet-occupied Germany very much as a rancher would shift herds of cattle or sheep on some drought-stricken tract of pasture — expecting and regretting loss in the move from starvation, disease, exhaustion and exposure, but hoping to achieve a minimum overall wastage.

Once active Fascists had been rounded up and liquidated in the Russian zone, Stalin's men were not pernickety enough to waste time and energy on the small fry. They put them to work at the job they were best capable of doing, and in the main rewarded them according to their merits. If later evidence disclosed that some of the people working under the new regime had been enthusiastic Nazis, then they were liquidated without fuss or bother — but not until less suspect workmen became available. The Russians took trouble to preserve for public trial at Nuremberg or elsewhere only war criminals whose punishment would have propaganda value. They dealt with the small-town bullies, low-calibre sadists and cranks, quietly and immediately, not caring too much about possible mis-carriages of justice. They were consistent in preferring the proletariat. Rank, wealth or class could gain no privileges for a German under Russian military rule. The only German who could expect preferment was a technician, an expert in some pure or applied science.

Next to the Russians, the British were quickest to realise that any attempt at moral therapy on the Germans was foredoomed to failure unless some sort of economic stability had first been achieved. After a few weeks' experience in northern Germany, the British Military Government gave up any serious effort to discriminate against anyone but men with the most notorious political records — men whose retention in offices of responsibility would have caused a downright international scandal.

With traditions and long experience of the administration of subject peoples behind them, the British were perhaps the best equipped of all the victors to get Germany on its feet economically. It had long been part of the British method to retain as many 'native institutions' as possible and to confirm 'native chieftains' in power, provided only they were willing in future to acknowledge British overlordship. After a few half-hearted experiments with formulae prepared by the military government division of SHAEF, this method was the one finally adopted by the majority of British military government officers in Germany. They were convinced that building a *new* Germany out of the debris of the old would be bothersome and probably impossible. Therefore they set about salvaging essential parts of the old order and encouraging the Germans themselves to assemble and get the machinery working again — the machinery they had perfected once before and with which they were so familiar. If the appointment of a man who had done a job well enough to please Hitler was not too blatant an affront to the ideal of punishing the wicked Nazis, he was put back in his old billet and told to do the job well enough to please Montgomery. Indeed, Montgomery's several announcements to the Germans in the British Zone of occupation might, with little simplification of language and alteration of reference, have been the proclamations of any senior officer of the armed forces of the King-Emperor to any tribe of bare-bottomed savages who had troubled the outposts of Empire and been conquered for their own good.

It was astonishing how quickly this system achieved results. When towards the end of 1945 I visited key points in the four zones, the British had undoubtedly progressed farthest towards restoration of normality. People were at work. They had regained a little confidence. Whether they approved of the British or not, they at least knew what to expect of them.

Of all occupying Powers, the Americans showed themselves the most inept at the business of governing a conquered country. They maintained little or no continuity of policy. They never succeeded in making up their minds whether they wanted to administer stern justice or indulge Christ-like charity. They did not, indeed, make up their minds about anything except the 'superiority' of their own intentions. Germans must be ruthlessly disciplined into loving and respecting liberty. They must be punished for their crimes as a nation, but innocent women and children must on no account suffer. German industrialists who were guilty of warmongering and supporting Hitler must be dispossessed, but on no account should collective ownership — Communism — be the result of that dispossession. The American Military Government must not involve the United States in the messy byways of European politics, but Europe must, of course, be prevented at all costs from going Red!

The unhappy executives of this American 'policy' in Germany were set to work for the achievement of all these inimical aims, vigorously and simultaneously; but as soon as they made progress in one direction, they were instantly restrained by torrents of criticism that they were making no progress in the other direction.

What happened in Bavaria in June and July was typical.

Bavaria had been the cradle of Nazism; yet if any German province could be said to have escaped complete domination by the Nazi idea, Bavaria was that province.

When the Americans moved into Munich, they found that one or two shadowy counter-Nazi organisations existed. Anti-Nazis had given trivial help to the invaders by removing roadblocks from the path of tank columns. A more considerable resistance, however, had been made by the clergy and prominent adherents of the Roman Catholic Church, led by the redoubtable prelate and politician, Cardinal Faulhaber.

ORIGINAL FINAL
CHAPTER, 1945
MANUSCRIPT

In the spring and summer of 1945, five million foreign soldiers marched into Germany. These were the men who saw the realities of victory, or at least the realities of material conquest. One had no way of knowing for certain their opinion of their own achievement, but few of the thousands to whom the newspaper correspondents talked, seemed to think that any major doubt had been settled by the war. The war had been fought in the spirit of disillusion. It had been fought only because it *had* to be fought; and when it was won, disillusion remained.

A philosophically-minded POW from one of the big *Lagers* near Regensburg best described the common malaise when he repeated an old observation: 'You know, this world is full of people who are willing to die fighting against something evil, but there are damned few who are willing to die fighting for something good.'

In October, my own assignment in Europe ended. I flew from Nuremberg for the last time. One thing struck me very forcibly as I looked down on the forests and fields and ruined cities: Germany, and more than 60 million Germans, were still there. That seemed to me to be a more important truth in the long run than the truth that Germany and more than 60 million Germans had been disorganised and disarmed and subjugated by the combined effort of 300 million British and Americans and Russians. Whether or not such an idea was acceptable to the excited minds of people who savoured the victory vicariously — twenty miles across the English Channel, or three hundred miles across the Atlantic, or eight hundred miles across the plains of Russia — Germany and the Germans would somehow or other outlive their subjugation. The men of the armies of occupation knew that from the beginning. Looking at them — men whose prospect of heroic vindication was now gone — I used to wonder what lessons they had learnt, what opinions they had formed, from fighting and winning the war. What faith had they gained from survival, or wisdom from authority?

If I had remained with them, I might have gone on with the business of looking for the truth, recording question and answer. But I did not stay with them. There was still myself to examine. I felt it was time to answer my own questionnaire.

Q: What is your most sure conclusion after witnessing the end of the European war and the beginning of European reconstruction?

A: I am convinced that winning the war imposed far less strain upon the genius of the victorious nations that winning the peace will impose. The military defeat of Nazism has by no means secured peace, justice or liberty for men. And I doubt that it has decided even an inconsiderable fraction of the issues which common men hoped, and were assured, it would decide.

Q: But surely there was a right side and a wrong side in the war, and the right triumphed? Wasn't it fought because something went wrong with the Germans as members of the human family?

A: I wish I could believe that, but I cannot. I believe there was a right and wrong, but not that the right side was wholly right, nor that Germany was wholly guilty.

Q: Why?

A: Something seems to have gone wrong with the human family as a whole. In the first place, I do not think that the great majority of Germans wanted the war. I am inclined to accept what they protest: that not 1 in 10 000 actually wanted the war. Yet Germany deliberately prepared for war, waged war — and waged it with a strength and fury that came within an ace of achieving world conquest — against the wishes of the great majority of Germans as individuals.

By the same token, I don't believe that the great majority of Germans wanted their criminal regime, or wanted a government that was responsible for the murder and torture of millions. Yet they supported that government by superhuman effort to the very end. That indicates what is wrong with humanity. A human herd can apparently pursue a certain course of action — and pursue it with vigour and success — even though that course of action is at variance with the conscience, desires and intelligent beliefs of the great majority of its individual members. That is where the war guilt of the United Nations comes in. After the last war, most people believed in the necessity for a League of Nations. They wanted it to work. Another war was an outrage to the human conscience. No intelligent man believed it either desirable or necessary. Yet in spite of conscience, desire and belief, the League failed and war came. Herds go their own way, irrespective of what the individuals in them are thinking.

Q: *Then you claim that the sum of individual moral beliefs is incapable of influencing the behaviour of the herd?*

A: Experience seems to show that the material condition of the herd in relation to other herds — its wants, its instinctive effort to achieve supremacy in the competition for material things — is more capable of weakening or changing individual moral beliefs than the sum of individual moral beliefs is capable of influencing herd behaviour. Herd pressure, long enough applied, makes warriors of many convinced pacifists.

Q: *And do you hold the German herd primarily responsible for the disaster that has befallen Europe?*

A: Yes, I think it primarily responsible. There is no other opinion to be drawn from the evidence.

Q: *Do you, therefore, believe that the German herd must be punished and controlled for its aberration into paths of wanton aggression and inhumanity both to assure its neighbours against any aberration in the future and to warn other herds?*

A: Punishment and control are not the same thing. It is not possible to 'punish' a herd. You can beat, starve or maltreat it, weaken its strength; but the herd as a herd is insensate. The herd does not suffer under punishment, only the individuals that make it up.

There are few people in Germany who feel — or who can ever be made to feel — that they have an individual responsibility for the war. Punishment of them as individuals (excepting those who personally committed crimes of inhuman cruelty and violence) will achieve less than nothing. It will merely rouse in them hatred, resentment and an ever-growing desire for retaliation. The herd can learn nothing from suffering inflicted on individuals, but control is another matter. I believe that Germany must be controlled.

Q: *How?*

A: By the same means whereby every other nation must be controlled if civilisation is to be preserved — made possible even — if the human species is to continue to exist.

Q: *Do you mean that Germany must not now be discriminated against?*

A: I can see no solution for Europe's problems in discrimination against Germany. The world does not need that. It needs discrimination — and effective discrimination — against the destructive elements that are to be found in all nations. From what I could learn of the anatomy of Nazism, from my own observation and the experience of those who suffered most under it, the elements which went to make it up are not peculiar to Germany. Under certain conditions Nazism could spring up in almost any country in the world. The name and superficial symptoms might be different, but it would be the same thing: gangster rule under the mast of inspirational nationalism; soulless regimentation justified by plea of expediency; coercion of a people by a governmental system of destroying all alternatives; government by fear-machine.

Q: *Under what conditions could Nazism rise again?*

A: Under the conditions that prevailed in Germany after the last war. It could arise under conditions of economic chaos, from the exploitation of the mass of the population by sectional interests, from moral exhaustion, from political inefficiency and corruption. Despair was the mother of Nazism.

Q: *Then you don't believe that there is something inherently evil in the German race, in the German herd, which menaces European and world peace?*

A: It is not a question of belief. No man has the right to a belief in such a matter. I have only an opinion. Nothing I have seen in Germany convinces me that there is anything peculiarly evil in the German herd. There are unlovely aspects in it, weakness, susceptibilities, but nothing peculiarly and inherently evil.

Q: *Not even in the concentration camps?*

A: I cannot forget that some of the most inhuman cruelties in the concentration camps were perpetrated by people not of German blood — by Frenchmen, Poles, Czechs, Hungarians, Russians. I was told this by camp prisoners. I wanted to find out how the camps were staffed — how as a simple proposition in human selection. I think I found out, and I believe that enough people to staff concentration camps could be found in any country. More particularly could concentration camps be staffed in countries where perversion has be propagated by fear, poverty, social disorder and repression. I cannot forget that people of my own race, only a century ago, flogged soldiers and sailors to death for trivial offences against discipline; slowly starved and worked to death many thousands in the 'concentration camps' of nineteenth-century factories and mines. The only unique aspect of German concentration camps is that they were a part of the governmental system in a modern, powerful state — established with deliberate intent to murder and torture. That state has now been destroyed.

Q: *Then you would advocate the forgiveness of Germany?*

A: Forgiveness is not the point. If I could advocate anything, I would advocate perpetuation of the hatred in which Nazism was held. I would like to see that hatred an ever-burning flame in the hearts and minds of all men. I would like to see a universal alertness to recognise Nazism wherever it might be found and under whatever mask and name.

Q: *But would the mere recognition of Nazism and continuing hatred of the wrongs against which men fought in this war constitute a practical political solution of the problem of Germany, Europe and the world?*

A: As a newspaper man, I have been professionally interested in political 'solutions' for nearly twenty years. I no longer see politics as a motivating force in human affairs. I see politics rather as an expression of human conditions. Parliamentary democracy is an expression of the condition of the British people in their relation to the world. With tragic outcome, Nazism was an expression of the condition of the German people in their relation to the world between the two wars.

Q: *Then you think that an effort to re-educate the German people politically cannot succeed?*

A: What is 'political education'? If the political re-education of Germany means converting the majority of Germans to belief in the system of parliamentary democracy, then I think conversion will come only

when the economic condition of Germany is healthy
and stable enough to support such a system. It is surely
not mere accident that the only countries in the world
which have long subscribed to parliamentary
democracy are countries possessing very great
economic advantages. And it is notable that when those
economic advantages are offset by the crisis of war,
there is and must be an immediate cancellation of most
of the liberties enjoyed by the individual under
democracy. Parliamentary democracy is a luxury. It can
be afforded, so far, only by the well endowed, by the
historically fortunate. Germany may evolve to it, just as
the rest of Europe may evolve to it, if technological
advances can achieve freedom from want for the have-
not nations. But it will not be grafted by projects of
forcible re-education into the way of life of any nation.

Q: *So, from what you have seen, you think that the military
occupation of Germany is doomed to failure in its major
objective?*

A: Military occupation of Germany was necessary to
complete the disarmament of a defeated foe. It was
necessary for the attempt to liquidate people who had
committed peculiarly horrible crimes against humanity.
It was necessary as a humanitarian measure because,
when the Nazi Government was obliterated, no
alternative administration existed to provide a regime
of order for more than 60 million living Germans. But
beyond these functions, I believe it is doomed to failure.
It will teach the Germans nothing except to hate, resent
and plot against foreigners. It will fortify rather than
destroy fanatical nationalism, because fanaticism
thrives on suppression as greatly as it thrives on power.
Nazism was discredited and destroyed by conquest, but
its ghost may be conjured up by alien intervention. The
German people will forget Belsen and Buchenwald and
Dachau, which few of them saw; but they will
remember the horror of the Berlin railway stations and

the Russian rape of a score of towns and cities, which millions of them saw. They will remember the children who died of hunger and disease and cold in the winter of 1945–46. They will forget the lies of Goebbels and the boasts of Goering, but they will remember the words which presaged a time of famine and black hopelessness and humiliation — Eisenhower's words, 'WE COME AS CONQUERORS'. They will remember the days of Nazism as stern days, full of discipline and effort and hope, however false. But they will know the days of occupation as days of repression and idleness and despair. They will forget the comparable misery their own occupation brought to France and Poland and the Low Countries, but they will remember well-fed British and American sailing boats on the Berlin lakes, and well-filled cookhouse scrap cans from which the guards drove back begging women and old men. Such remembering and such forgetfulness is part of all human nature. It is not peculiar to Germans.

Q: *Surely, if that is a valid opinion, the men who had at their command genius great enough to win the war, are aware of the truth?*

A: I believe they are aware of the truth. But the men who today lead nations are themselves, like their politics, effects rather than causes. They, too, are symptomatic of the condition of the herds they lead. The nations which united to deal with the common danger of militant Fascism in Europe and militant imperialism in Asia were united only by that danger. In common emergency, differences of condition were overlooked, but now that the emergency has passed the differences were again agonisingly apparent, intensified rather than diminished by the strain of war. When the battles were over, the great Allied Powers found they really had in common only one thing: a stake in the carcass of prostrate Germany and certain unsubstantial sentiments of wartime comradeship.

I don't believe the men of intelligence and capacity who lead the United Nations today, seriously expect the military occupation of Germany, or its economic and territorial partitioning to contribute anything to the cause of peace. I believe rather that they are fully aware that the continued occupation and the forcible partitioning of Germany will constitute a continual menace to peace. But they cannot admit this or withdraw unilaterally, because unilateral admission and withdrawal would mean giving up the immediate material and political advantages they hope to derive from remaining. The condition of each herd is such that it dislikes, distrusts and fears the others, and is therefore unwilling to yield them advantages.

Q: *But what material and political advantages can the Allies derive from continued occupation of Germany?*

A: Materially, loot at worst and 'reparations' at best. The Russians want machinery and technicians. They have been taking them and will continue as long as there are technicians and machinery to take. I personally investigated reports that large quantities of German machinery were being removed to Russia to replace Russian machinery destroyed during the German invasion. I was satisfied they were correct, and later open admission was made by the Russians. I also personally investigated reports that the Russians were kidnapping German technicians, and was satisfied that they, too, were substantially correct, although sometimes exaggerated.

The Americans also want German processes and technicians. They are taking both, though not under duress. They have no need to use duress. Technicians in the Zeiss works in Jena boasted to me that they had excellent prospects of jobs in America 'until things quietened down'.

In a broader sense, America has, or believes it has, a great deal to gain by the elimination of German industry as a competitor in the world markets of tomorrow. The American economic system is inherently expansionist, and it can continue to operate only by stimulating and exploiting foreign markets.

Britain, too, is undoubtedly interested in the elimination of German industrial competition, although as far as I could find out it has not taken much part directly in the looting of German technical resources.

France tacitly admits that it wants the loot of the Rhineland and Ruhr. It wants access to the coal, iron and heavy industries of the Rhine Valley on its own terms — terms handsomely profitable to the French economic order whenever France can again claim to have an economic order.

Politically and strategically, the advantages to be gained from competitive intervention in Germany are equally clear. Russia, profoundly shocked by her narrow escape from defeat in 1941, wants a protective 'apron' of dependent Communist states in the Balkans and Central Europe. It is actively communising its own zone of occupation in Germany and clandestinely assisting the organisation of Communist factions in the British and American zones. In this case the political graft will take. Economic disorganisation and distress provide suitable conditions for the growth of Communism.

Britain, whose state has been expressed by a switch to Democratic Socialism, is afraid that it will be at a grave disadvantage in trying to deal with an all-Communist Europe. It is doing all it can to prevent the communisation of Germany, even to the extent of neglecting the objective, publicly proclaimed sacred, of de-Nazifying German local government and industry. All over the British zone I found evidence of the employment of men who had cooperated with Hitler's Government. In part, this was due to expediency, but expediency fitted in with the British plan. Loosely, the British strategy is to attempt the restoration of some sort of industrial stability and prosperity before Communism becomes inevitable as the result of prolonged disorder and distress.

The United States have no direct political stake in Europe, but the nation's involvement in two European wars has shown that it has a stake in world affairs, whether or not it likes the idea. American industrialists were convinced that they couldn't do business with an all-Nazi Europe, or Japanese-dominated Asia. Therefore the nation fought. American industrialists are now convinced that they will not be able to do profitable business with an all-Communist Europe, and they are fighting the Communists with every weapon they dare use in a world physically exhausted and morally revolted by open war.

Anti-Soviet propaganda is intense among American troops of the armies of occupation. The propaganda is fully effective only because of the differences of custom, language and background between American and Russian troops. Moreover, the Russian troops and their commanders, still suffering from a historical inferiority complex, are suspicious, stubbornly uncooperative, secretive, and lose no opportunity, however trivial, of 'getting the advantage' of the British and Americans.

The Americans are using, or trying to use, Roman Catholicism in Germany to fight the Communists just as the British are using, or trying to use, the remnants of the industrial hierarchy of the Ruhr and north Germany to restore capitalism.

The French, without any real influence or defined ideology, hope to get at least part of their material demands by auctioning their moral support and sentimental prestige.

No. I don't believe that the stated objectives of the occupation of Germany — reformation, rehabilitation, and insurance against future war — are true objectives. The occupation so far has shown no real progress towards either reformation or rehabilitation. The statesmen of Europe know it. Furthermore, the occupation as it is now developing will increase rather than diminish the danger of war, because it is nothing more or less than a way of bargaining for the spoils accrued from the defeat and dismemberment of a great European power. The statesmen know this, too.

Q: *Is there any solution, then? Or do you believe that the inequality of herds will once more plunge Europe and the world into a conflict which the majority of individuals feel certain will destroy the civilisation they know?*

A: I believe that the solution lies only in the making and enforcing of a code of laws which will bind nations as effectively as existent laws bind the individuals within a community of civilised men. Laws cannot be made to bind a selected few. They must, to endure, bind all.

In no community of civilised men can one individual retain sovereignty above the law. So it must be in a community of civilised nations. That is the lesson, the only worthwhile lesson, that can be learnt from the terror and waste and cruelty of the years just past. A score of million people have died in the search for the touchstone that will make a law for nations practicable. I cannot and will not believe, remembering those dead and the living who still strive, that my kin will fail in the search, or in the end reject truth.

Q: *Is there any evidence to support your belief that men will not reject truth, and that in the end they will find what they are searching for?*

A: Only the evidence that they have contrived continuity of existence for hundreds of thousands of years, mastering their environment more and more surely as time went on, until at last man is his own environment. Can man now master himself? That is the question only time can answer. There is hope at least in the fact that the question has been clearly put, by the war and the atom bomb. The ultimate enemy is known.

GLOSSARY OF TERMS

C rations	*canned field ration of the US Army*
CO	*commanding officer*
CP	*command post*
DP	*displaced persons*
G2	*US Army Intelligence Group*
Herrenvolk	*master race*
K rations	*packaged, emergency field ration of the US armed forces*
Lager	*camp*
Lebensraum	*literally, 'living space'; territory claimed by a nation or state on the grounds that it is necessary for survival or growth*
Luftschutzraum	*air-raid shelter*
MG	*(Allied) Military Government*
MP	*military police*
OKW	*Oberkommando der Wehrmacht*
Oberkommando	*Supreme Command*
PFC	*Private, First Class*
POW	*prisoner of war*
PX	*post exchange*
RAF	*Royal Air Force*
S mine	*German anti-personnel mine*
SHAEF	*Supreme Headquarters Allied Expeditionary Force*
snafu	*situation normal all fouled up*
SP gun	*self-propelled gun*
TD	*tank destroyers*
Volkssturm	*German territorial army*